Dear Miss Landau ...

Juliet Landau

Dear Miss Landau ...

JAMES CHRISTIE

CHAPLIN BOOKS

www.chaplinbooks.co.uk

First published in 2012 by Chaplin Books
Copyright © James Christie

ISBN 978-0-9565595-6-2

A CIP catalogue record for this book is available from The British Library.

Design by The Better Book Company, Chichester
Printed in the UK by Ashford Colour Press

Cover design by Helen Taylor

Chaplin Books
1 Eliza Place
Gosport PO12 4UN
Tel: 023 9252 9020
www.chaplinbooks.co.uk

Most men lead lives of quiet desperation,
and go to their graves with the song still in them.

Henry David Thoreau

Angel: *Well, if you're lonely, Dru, why don't you make yourself*
             a playmate?

Drusilla: *I could! I could pick the wisest and bravest knight in*
             all the land and make him mine forever with a kiss.

Darla: *Or you could just take the first drooling idiot that*
             comes along...

Angel

James Christie

Foreword

My father was born in India where he learned the ways of Islam. He once taught me a saying of the Prophet Muhammad, and the words have always stayed with me:

Allah the Merciful the Compassionate, weaves the threads of men's destinies into many strange tapestries.

From a row of Scottish tenements, the threads of my destiny would draw me across an ocean and 3,000 miles of hard road to a street in Los Angeles, a state reserve south of Carmel and a meeting on a boulevard west of Sunset.

With my mother Ethne Mary on Ilkley Moor, 1965.
She gave me my middle name of Anthony
after the patron saint of travellers...

And of lost souls...

1

Alien

"Know your limitations."

It was kindly advice, given by a decent man in a grey consulting room in Drumchapel, a poor district west of Glasgow.

He was a psychologist. I was his subject, and he had just diagnosed me with Asperger Syndrome – a form of autism. It was the reason why, despite a higher education and an IQ of 134, I had had great difficulty holding down a decent job and the chance of getting a girlfriend seemed as far from me as a Viking's Valhalla. And if there is a sunlit city on a hill waiting for us (or in the case of a Viking, a flaming longship pushed out to sea by several scantily-clad Norsewomen), it felt a million miles distant from a depressed part of Glasgow on a drab day in the early autumn of 2002.

I'd been a long time getting there, with many a humiliation on the way. I'd been analysed before, by a friend of my father's with a personality-profiling business, but although he'd had some perceptive insights, he had not really been able to get to the root of the problem. Autism as we know it today was first defined in 1943 but Asperger Syndrome, its milder variant, was not recognised until 1981. Autism is a broad spectrum disorder. None who suffer from it show every one of its varied symptoms, but all Autists (as I shall call my strange brotherhood) share a few universal attributes:

1)   a 'differently-wired' brain. Typical human beings (known in the trade as neuro-typicals or NTs) think emotionally first and logically afterwards – sometimes quite a long time afterwards – but Autists are the other way round. We think logically first and emotionally next. Call it the 'Mr Spock Concept'

and think of the way he and Dr McCoy used to spar verbally:

"Really, Dr McCoy, you must learn to govern your passions. They will be your undoing. Logic suggests..."

"You green-blooded, inhuman..."

(*Star Trek II: The Wrath of Khan*)

There, in a nutshell, are the neuro-typical and autistic mindsets sparring with each other, the passionate, emotional human and the logical (autistic) Vulcan. But it is important to remember that neuro-typical humans can think logically and autistic Vulcans do have emotions. Autists can indeed love, which leads me to point two:

2)   Difficulty in communicating and with social interaction. Put another way (and with the bluntness typical of Autists, who do not always realise that their logical statements can cause emotional embarrassment), I was 31 before I first had sex and in my forties before I'd taught myself how to manage socially and relate to women. Since they are apparently from Venus and I was a Vulcan, you can perhaps imagine the problems.

Logical autism did proffer certain advantages, though. I was a sexual inadequate for so long that I had been forced, seriously and *logically*, to come to terms with and control my male ego. So when I did finally manage to pick up some pretty obvious hints from a pretty inebriated woman, I just did my best, tried to remember the rules, and gave her as good a time as possible. I was pleased to discover I was quite good at it.

3)   Difficulty with social imagination. My old school reports regularly said I was 'away in my own world', so I had to learn how to prise myself out of my shell and relate to others. NTs pick up the unwritten rules of social life

automatically, but I had to teach myself manually and consciously remind myself that other people were just as flawed, neurotic and inadequate as I was. They were just better at concealing it...

Up to that point then, my life had not been a complete failure, so I listened equably, fairly unemotionally, and with some relief, as my psychologist finally explained to me why sex, social relationships and the never-ending need to learn, learn, learn had been such trials for me. Why I had had a few too many career stumbles, why I could not take in and process information with the ease of my neuro-typical siblings, and why I could not reliably pick up NT females' subtle signals.

Why? Because they *weren't* my siblings and never had been. After 37 years, I finally knew who I actually was. An Autist. Mr Spock. Differently wired. *Alien.*

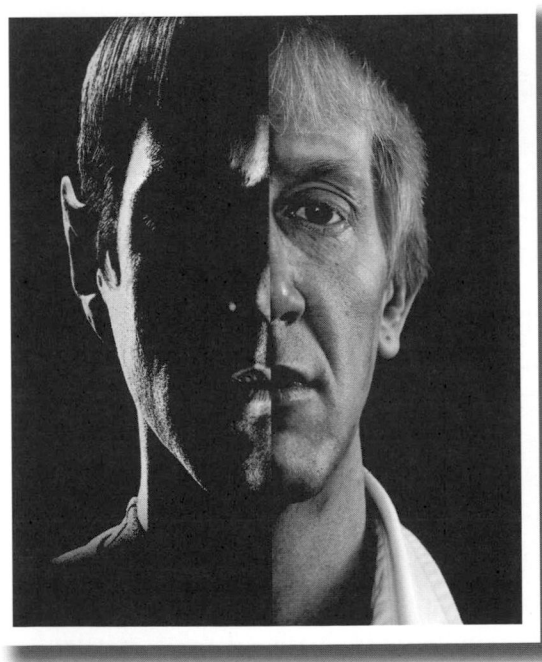

A Vulcan, adrift amidst humans

It was really quite exciting: a whole new perspective from which to view the world. You think this planet is crazy? It probably is. Blame the emotionally driven, egotistical, illogical neuro-typicals running it.

"Your verbal IQ is within the top 1 percent of the population," my psychologist went on, "but your performance IQ is only in the top 39 percent. This is a significant and unusual difference. You have a major deficit in processing speed, that is to say your ability to quickly and efficiently process visual information, and the speed at which you learn, is better than only 3 percent of the population."

"You mean," I said, processing the information slowly, "that I'm part near genius, part low-grade moron? In the top 1 percent in one area, in the bottom 3 percent in the other?"

"I wouldn't put it quite that bluntly, Mr Christie..."

"I would. I'm an Autist."

"If we think of your brain as a computer, its processor is not really up to the job of powering all your software programs. It's as if wildly obsolete Amstrad hardware had to run Windows 2000. Think how hard such a processor would have to work to make all those programs function."

"And yet my verbal IQ – my articulacy and writing ability – is very superior?"

"Yes. Other people no doubt judge you on your superior verbal abilities and make no allowance for what are very hidden problems. Hidden from you as well as from them."

"It's terribly frustrating. They expect me to do what they seem so effortlessly able to do, and turn on me when I can't."

I didn't feel so excited any more. Time and again, I'd been offered a glimpse of the sunlit city on the hill, and time and again the chance had been snatched from me. Now at least I knew why, but the bitterness and humiliation were still with me, and I could not be 'cured.' A computer's processor could be replaced, but a human brain could not be rewired.

Well, not without killing me, anyway.

I later learnt from another Autist just how hard my 'processor' or central processing unit (CPU) would have to work to communicate and socialise:

> *"I've spent my life learning how to 'read' people using conscious thought ... after twenty-seven years of this I have become skilled at reading people. Unlike NT folks, this is a conscious effort and requires considerable energy, but it works and I can often 'see' things NT people would never see in negotiations. The only downside of this is that negotiations are absolutely exhausting for me. I think I do a good job of appearing 'normal' on the surface, but I am actually burning through incredible amounts of CPU cycles trying to read the other people."*

(Barbara Jacobs, *Loving Mr Spock*, p.85)

I also found out that, if it was a car engine, the neuro-typical brain could cruise through the day at 2,000 rpm, pretty much on autopilot. I began to suspect that my own brain had a much less effective autopilot, so in order to get through a normal day I would have to rev my brain up to 4,000 rpm.

Ironically, it seemed Mr Spock's brain worked this way, too. In the *Star Trek* episode *Spock's Brain*, Dr McCoy commented that, *"Spock's body is much more dependent than ours on that tremendous brain of his for life support."*

So I would have to struggle through the day with a tiring brain under manual control, thinking out what to do, not trusting my emotional instincts, feeling like Mr Spock (who, incidentally, has an Asperger's body language) on a shipful of NTs. Dependent on the tremendous parts of my brain to compensate for the deficient areas, knowing that if the engine started to run hot the software would seize up. Realising that, like Spock, I was adrift in a sea of aliens I did not understand, and who did not understand me.

No, not so exciting after all.

Still, I did have a degree in creative writing, a postgraduate diploma in librarianship, chartered membership of the Library

Association, a job as librarian for a law firm and a flat in the best part of town. Even my psychologist had assumed I lived at home with my mother and I'd quite enjoyed telling him I actually had a job and a flat in the city.

But the job and flat had been hard won. In those days, only about 15 percent of Autists were in full-time employment, mainly because we were natural backroom boys in a frontline world. Have you ever noticed how the media goes on about 'frontline services', usually with reference to doctors and nurses? It's an ignorant cry, but typical of the world of NT employment where the attributes of sociability, flexibility and networking are king, and where emotion often comes well before logic. Managers want to prove their manhood by making their organisations 'lean and mean' – usually by concentrating on frontline services, firing the backroom boys and only then realising they've destroyed their supply chain and knowledge base.

In such a world, Autists are like fish out of water. Very few can find a respectable position where their talents can be used and very many either never get into the pool at all or are thrown mercilessly out of the water and left gasping in the unforgiving air.

Some of those things I knew then, on that drab, exciting day in 2002. Some I had still to learn.

I shook my psychologist's hand. I might be underpaid, under-used and unappreciated, I thought to myself, but I was still swimming around productively and in a stroke I'd gone from an underperforming neuro-typical to an exceptionally high functioning Autist. One who could shake people's hands and look them in the eye, no less. Now, though, I was beginning to know my limitations, so in the future I would surely be able to avoid the stumbles and humiliations which had dogged me in the past?

Surely, as they sang on the day of Tony Blair's election victory, things could only get better?

2

An autistic Reginald Perrin

"We're *not* buying any more shelving."

I looked at Madame Scrooge, the assistant practice director of my new law firm, where I was working for a salary which would bring tears to the eyes of the hardest man in the Scottish Low Pay Unit.

My former law firm (whom I'd liked a great deal) had made me redundant two weeks before Christmas 2001. They had wanted to replace their tired old personnel manager with a new, freshly minted human resources director.

"Do that and I'll take you to an employment tribunal," said she to the partners. So instead they got rid of *me* and gave her my job, falling all over themselves all the while to reassure me it had had nothing to do with the quality of my work.

And merry Christmas to you too, you bunch of...

Scots do not like to be accused of being Scrooges but sometimes the clichés are true. My new firm was carpeted in burnt ochre baked dry by an overzealous heating system which filtered any humour out of the place. In the wake of a bumpy merger the partners were at war with each other and, worst of all, not one move could be made – ever – without costing, costing and more costing.

I only had two days a week to fix the back room (or more precisely, the library) which had been left to rot for years. Even after the bookstock was weeded there would still be three times as many books as there was shelving available, and new books also had to be bought because the law changes with extraordinary speed.

Those were unequivocal facts clear to an Autist, but try telling that to the not-very-bright Madame Scrooge, who (as the tea lady told me *sotto voce*) had been turned down for the post six times in seven years. With good reason. On the seventh attempt they let her in, and I bet they regret it still.

They would not part with money, thinking (like neuro-typicals) that there must be some way round the problem. Some magical way which didn't involve spending money or facing up to inconvenient and unpleasant truths which did not mesh with their viewpoints.

There wasn't. There simply was not enough shelving available in the building upon which to stack the books. I made this plain to Madame Scrooge. Her eyes screwed up and through pursed lips, shot out like an expletive, came that sentence:

"We're *not* buying any more shelving."

I took pyrrhic revenge in the end. Madame Scrooge minced along one day (I think I remember flowers wilting in their vases as she passed) and asked me if I could "just fit the books in."

I hesitated for a moment, thinking of the way I, the supposedly inflexible Autist, had thought laterally but come up with nothing, while trying to meet this halfwit halfway to find a workable solution.

Madame Scrooge. The supposedly flexible neuro-typical, standing there as rigid and dense as a pillar.

I thought about my response for a moment. Was there any way, any way at all, this could actually be done?

There wasn't. It wasn't even a case of putting a pint-and-a-half into a pint pot. It was *three* pints. And besides, I'd had it. I had spent four years proving myself at my previous firm, whose problems were identical, and I was fed up to my back teeth with trying to talk logical but unpopular sense to managers driven by emotion, ego and illogic.

"No" I said, careful not to qualify my answer one iota.

Madame Scrooge pursed her lips to a prodigious degree and left. Shortly thereafter, so did I. Permanently. By then, I had been struggling to deal with neuro-typicals in the public and private sectors for 16 years and my patience was at an end. I felt like an autistic version of Reginald Perrin, sick of Sunshine Desserts and ready to throw off my clothes, jump into the English Channel, fake my own death and start a new life.

I was relieved to be able to express my frustrations to my psychologist in Drumchapel (fortunately without throwing my clothes off), and to get the opportunity to train for a job with a cataloguing agency in the country.

I was also lucky to become a client of the National Autistic Society Scotland (NAS), and luckier than I knew to meet Jim Doherty of Prospects, the Society's employment arm. Jim was the best of men, and now I was walking down a new and unexpected road, the first to guide me along the way.

Autists are particularly well-suited to jobs which involve filing, cataloguing and indexing. I had previous cataloguing experience, wanted to get out of the city and hoped to achieve my life's ambition of earning a poverty-level salary of £15,000 per annum.

I would be 40 by the time my training in cataloguing was complete. Hopefully, life would then begin.

3

Naturally pernickety

"We're *not* giving you a contract."

I'd slogged away diligently at the cataloguing agency for nine months, let my Glasgow flat to a tenant, moved most of the flat's contents to the family home in South Lanarkshire, rented a room in the local town, and as those words were delivered unto me by a not-unsympathetic managing director, I realised it had all been for nothing.

It may seem I write this as if relocating had been an easy set of transactions. For an Autist, it was nothing of the sort. It was hell and damnation, and I think I'd rather have been chained to a rock with a vulture pecking out my liver on a daily basis.

This was because Autists do not like variations in routine and need time to adjust to change. Time to rev up the tiring brain and overcome the inertia which threatens to overwhelm us. After two years sleeping on a mattress in the lounge, I'd just got my flat in order. I'd carefully designed it to be autism-friendly, with everything tidy and in its place, and I'd nicknamed it 'Asperger World.' Now, with my own hands, I had had to tear it down, and that felt worse than smashing my own head through a plate-glass window.

Think of trying to find your way along a path blocked by sharp-edged metal boxes which smash against your ankles as you try to get through. Coping with and processing the sensory input necessary to plot your path through the day is a frustrating, blocky experience. The brain sags under the load and can get so tired that when people talk to you, you can hear the words but be unable to work out the meaning.

To then translate yourself into a new context and learn new skills is a fairly gruesome form of self-torture. Imagine

The Toll House at Roberton, about the time I learned I'd be cleaning toilets to pay my dues

smashing your ankles against sharp edges for half-an-hour or so, then climbing into a boxing ring and letting a heavyweight contender beat on your head for a while, and you've got some idea how hard it is for an Autist to change.

I had bashed my ankles against the boxes, let the contender beat on my head, and it had all been for nothing. I was 40, out of work, and a failure. It had been a bright dawn that day, when I thought I'd finally make the grade, but the cup (or rather the contract) had been dashed from my lips once again.

Librarianship should be the trade of choice for some Autists, because it always used to look for orderly, methodical people with a knack for detail. The type of person who liked routine, enjoyed cataloguing, jumped at the chance to shelve books in order and could focus on readers' enquiries.

However, there are hardly any job vacancies in libraries any more. Looking up the Library Association's jobs website, the average number of posts going in Scotland per month varies between two and six. That's two to six jobs in all of *Scotland,* not just Glasgow or Edinburgh.

Furthermore, a strange paradox seems to exist within the trade. To explain, a library cataloguer has to follow incredibly precise rules. Cataloguers, in a word, make accountants look like hippies. A cataloguer with Asperger Syndrome (like me) can follow these rules easily, but there seems to be an internet firewall in my brain. The part of my mind which has to deal with insanely pernickety and arbitrary rules *is kept firmly separate from my everyday personality*.

As a result, I managed to retain my perspective as well as the sense of humour every cataloguer needs, and my everyday personality was never infected with the pernickety obsessiveness every cataloguer also needs. Autists, in a word, are natural cataloguers. A naturally pernickety mind cannot be infected with pernicketiness. I do not think it is the same for neuro-typicals.

Librarianship was once a fine and honourable trade, but it seems to have become dominated by a bunch of obsessives determined to turn it into a 'profession' by complicating every aspect of it while using arcane jargon to argue endlessly with each other about what a librarian actually is, instead of trying to defend and promote the 'profession' itself.

Using the jargon of the library 'profession', I once constructed the following sentence:

> *While strange people in closed committee debate ways and means of animating the space to achieve a level of automated social tagging based on behavioural pathways using a user-endorsed system in order to negotiate a reference question in micro increments, Joe Public is begging for libraries dedicated to books.*

A missive which included that sentence was sent to *Update*, the library journal, and won letter of the month in May 2008...

Think of the Judean People's Front from Monty Python's *Life of Brian* and you'll get a good idea how out of touch senior librarians have become.

To paraphrase:

"They're arrested James the librarian! They've dragged him off. They're gonna crucify him!"

"Right! This calls for immediate discussion!"

"Reg, let's go now, please!"

"Right! Right! In the light of fresh information from sibling Juliet..."

"Reg, for God's sake! It's perfectly simple. All you've gotta do is go out of that door now and try to stop the Romans nailing him up! It's happening, Reg! Something's actually happening, Reg! Can't you understand?"

I wish I was joking. Tragically, a major potential source of employment for Autists has been ruined by neuro-typicals who, ironically, seem less able than myself to realise that obsessive behaviour can go too far.

The Dewey Decimal Classification System is an arbitrary, numerical method of classifying Mankind's entire body of knowledge. It was created by Melvil Dewey in 1876 and librarianship's senior, senile and sad obsessives have been over-complicating it ever since.

I came upon Dewey in 2004. I spent nine months struggling through insanely convoluted rules of number construction under the tutelage of a neuro-typical without a firewall, and her everyday personality had certainly been affected by Dewey. She lived in a shuttered house without TV, sounded like Nurse Ratched from *One Flew Over The Cuckoo's Nest*, and her favourite words were "you're wrong, you're wrong, and you're wrong." If she had been a horsewoman, she would have been a cruel rider, intent on digging silver spurs slowly and ever more deeply into her horse's shrinking flanks.

I often wove my way back to my digs in a speechless, battered funk, but hard as I tried, I could not construct Dewey numbers either quickly or efficiently enough. Coming up just a little bit short of an arbitrarily set, wilfully overcomplicated bar was also sheer psychological torture, with serious consequences for my fragile self-esteem. There was the terrible feeling that if

I had tried a little harder, if I had been just that little better as a person, then I could have reached the gates of the sunlit city, but I was never quite good enough and could only gaze at the silver spires from a distance. A sense of frustrated worthlessness was well-ensconced in my gut by then and the realisation that the work itself had no intrinsic value could not dislodge it. Hardly anyone knows what the Dewey number 781.640904803 means, and no-one cares.

So, no contract, no employment, no future and no belief left in my trade.

Only those who have been fired can know how it feels to see nothing ahead except an endless span of empty days, and I truly hate people who sit in safe jobs with no real understanding of autism yet tell me what I should do. Let them try it for themselves and see what it is like.

So what, then, could possibly come next?

All I did know was that two TV series I rather liked – *Buffy the Vampire Slayer* and its spin-off *Angel* – had just been cancelled. *Buffy* was slain in 2003 and *Angel* went to heaven in 2004.

At the end of April 2004, some of the *Buffy/Angel* cast attended a fan convention in Blackpool. At that time, I was beginning to browse through the internet during my lunch hours at the cataloguing agency, and came across an interview with a cast member on the BBC's website. Her name was Juliet Landau. I looked at her photograph for a moment, not knowing who she was, and not caring.

The relationship between the celebrity and the man in the street is, by definition, a strange one. At first, you (the man in the street) can see her (the celebrity), but she can't see you and that's usually the way it stays.

Usually.

4

Mr Spock's wisdom

I do not know whether there is a fate which shapes our ends, but as Mr Spock would say, *"there are always possibilities."*

I would catch a glimpse of heaven at Sunset, but I would have to go through hell to get there.

Autism has its advantages. An emotional neuro-typical might be unable to comprehend the hard fact that he was out of work, *sans* any future, and had wasted years of his life on a 'profession' which (as quite a few librarians had already told me) was dead on its feet.

Hard as they were, I had no difficulty comprehending those facts. I got the message. It was almost a relief to realise that my limitations could be pushed no further. I had always worked as quickly and efficiently as I could, but more than that I could not do.

So I had a choice. Go home to Mum and wallow happily in idleness, using Asperger's as an excuse; or pick myself up again and keep trying, armed this time with a darkly humorous acceptance of my limitations.

Not that much choice, really.

It wasn't all about neuro-typicality and autism, either. Character came into it, too. It would have been too easy to make excuses for myself. In the end, you can argue yourself out of doing anything, but I had seen enough of the Scottish public sector's 'ooh, we cannae do that' attitude to have any truck with it, and I come from an army family.

So get on your feet, young man, and stand up once more.

I went back to the benefits agency in Lanark, signed on the dole and started looking for work. I tried not to think of it as a stigma, tried to treat it as an administrative transaction, tried to use my humour and keep my perspective. I might still end up behind the eight-ball, but at least I would keep my dignity.

I got lucky, although I didn't think so at first. The Welcome Break Group had a motorway service area near my family home, they were always a tad understaffed and just a little desperate, so when they received a dog-eared job application from a dog-eared 40-year-old reject, they grabbed me like a shot. It was a refreshing change. For my entire life the supply of potential workers had *always* exceeded the demand, enabling organisations to cherry-pick.

Not so at this Welcome Break. They were in a beautiful, empty place with few cherries left on the local trees. They jumped at me and I accepted, with some reservations, a basic support crew job. At the age of 40, would I be able to cope with the manual work, and would I get on with my colleagues? I wasn't exactly going to be rubbing shoulders with graduates and I'd met some exceedingly nasty pieces of work in my time.

I had escaped the dole after only 17 days and I was on my feet, but the muscles were weary, the bones ached, and the enthusiasm of youth for the fray seemed long departed.

The future felt very uncertain, and for an Autist desperate for routine and security, that was hell.

5

The cleanest toilets in the country

"I know this sounds really naff," I said to one of my new colleagues some weeks later, "but I'd forgotten what a beautiful shade of bluc the sky is."

You never can tell how things will turn out. They were good people at the Welcome Break. They were all good people. The kind of people a schmaltzy writer might make into caricatures, sweet as sugar and dispensing homilies on a daily basis.

So no, they weren't quite like that. Nor was it much fun reminding my body how to work hard five days a week, but the muscle memory laid down in my younger days paid dividends. I could do the work, I bent to the wheel with a will, and the people accepted me.

The unexpected idyll, where I found peace amidst the toilets

It wasn't easy getting up at five to clean toilets at seven, and it might have seemed a comedown for a graduate to scrub out latrines and polish floors, but the robust body and something called 'Asperger focus' helped.

As a rough generalisation, Autists are better at concentrating on a single job while neuro-typicals are more able to multi-task. To be a bit catty about it, we are better at doing one job well than NTs are at doing many jobs badly, and we usually display a mildly relentless perfectionism.

That touch of slightly obsessive compulsiveness led to the cleanest toilets the support crew had seen in a while. My stock shot up. Younger people did not really want to do such work and those who had to usually complained at full throttle and only stuck around a short time. Nor (to be blunt) were there any cheerful, hard-working immigrants to fill the gap, because there was nowhere near as much accommodation available in the country as there was in the city. So the job was left to the ageing locals. The most senior man in the support crew was an ex-miner in his fifties, I was in my forties, and bringing up the rear was a former plasterer in his late thirties by the name of Gordon. I asked him once how he'd ended up at the Welcome Break.

"Fell off a roof," he said. "Broke my left wrist badly."

He raised his arm. I saw the joint, slightly swollen and a little crooked. Realised how, in one moment, he'd lost his trade and been forced to turn to emptying bins and sweeping up.

"People like us always end up here," he said levelly, not sorry for himself, just stating a fact.

There were people from Douglas and Abington and Crawford at the Welcome Break, from farms way out in the Lowther Hills, from the line of houses at the Daer Reservoir which were as far from anywhere as far could be, up beyond the green ridges of Forestry Commissioned pines. There were kids and students from over the Dalveen or Mennock Pass. There was a lady from Wales, a beauty from Moffat and a sweet young thing from Biggar. There was a cook who looked like a pirate from the Spanish Main and a former staff sergeant down from the Leadhills.

South Lanarkshire's Upper Clyde Valley is a funny old place. West of the Borders, north of Dumfries and Galloway, east of Ayrshire but in no way part of the Central Belt; and depending upon a person's point of view, either a dead-end depressed area or a rural Eden too often overlooked by tourists rushing to Edinburgh's Festival and the Highland line.

The valley's people melted all together in the Welcome Break's pot. The wages were low and the shifts long, but the air was clear and the work strangely satisfying.

I could not ignore the fact, though, that I'd left Glasgow to find a permanent job in my chosen 'profession', but the only permanent contract I'd been able to earn was one cleaning toilets. Such is the fate of many Autists.

I worked hard, made friends and recanted my prejudices. I'd got a bit sick of young people in Glasgow. The term 'ned' stands for non-educated delinquent and the dear green place had a fair few of *those*. At odd moments, there was a hint of violence in Glasgow's air. Although attitudes were changing and a café culture of coffee shops blooming, there were still too many pubs by far and the old clichés of racism and sectarianism still flowed like faeces under the surface.

The young of the Upper Clyde Valley were a different breed, with accents and attitudes softer than Glasgow, and with an innocence I prized, though it was combined with common sense and the rural version of street smarts.

Like an ageing engine, I was reconditioned. By autistic standards I was earning well, I had a permanent job, I enjoyed the free food dished out to employees at the Coffee Primo and I'd even known a little love.

And there was one other thing.

Sky One was showing reruns of *Buffy the Vampire Slayer* and, like a vampire's victim, it was putting me in its thrall.

Not perhaps for the reasons you might think. *Buffy's* creator, Joss Whedon, had turned the vampire genre's traditional conventions on their head by making a short, blonde girl – usually a silly, screaming stereotype polished off by Christopher

Lee as an apéritif before the battle royal between the befanged baddie and the handsome male hero – into the main protagonist.

One girl in all the world, chosen to fight the forces of darkness. Possessing extraordinary strength and reflexes, and in the case of Buffy Anne Summers, an irreverent wit masking a certain vulnerability.

Buffy the vampire slayer. Resident of Sunnydale, a small California town sited on the Hellmouth (a mystical convergence of evil forces), leader of the Scooby Gang (a collection of assorted local sidekicks who helped her fight evil), lover of Angel (the tormented vampire cursed with a soul and conscience, known as Angelus in his soulless incarnation) and Spike's object of desire. Spike, also known as William the Bloody, a soulless vampire with platinum hair, chiseled cheekbones, a dry wit and a serious case of the hots for his own nemesis.

Joss Whedon had the knack of being able to make the viewer care about his characters. He took the risk (rare in US broadcasting) of allowing his creations to grow, develop and explore their dark sides. Together with his talented team of writers, Whedon wrote a pilot followed by 144 multi-layered *Buffy* episodes which combined comedy, drama and tragedy in order to explore typical teenage issues within a fantastical context.

Some teenage girls think the world will end if they're not allowed to do their own thing. In Buffy's case, it just might.

So *Buffy the Vampire Slayer*, buoyed up by fine writing, sympathetic characters and a high thematic concept which harks back to tales of myth and legend from antiquity, won three Emmy awards and became one of the greatest TV series of all time.

Most TV shows, to be brutally honest, are either about cutting someone up (*ER*), arresting somebody (*Law & Order*), or arguing in court (*Perry Mason* to *The Good Wife*, and counting). *NCIS*, perhaps, does all three – finding someone who's been cut up, arresting the villain and then arguing about it in court…

Despite its hip dialogue and typical US high school setting, chock-full of beautifully coiffed teens sporting rows of achingly

Beautiful Dru, the tragic Ophelia to Spike's loudmouthed Hamlet

white teeth, *Buffy* told classic tales of high adventure. Of heroes and their ladies. Of knights and dragons, and quests for swords and grails.

Admittedly, Joss and his producer Marti Noxon did subvert the form with cheerful relish, making the hero a lady, the white knight a bit of a nerd and one of the dragons a conscience-stricken object of the lady's desire, but respected the genre as they did so. If Buffy was Arthur and the Scythe her Excalibur, then the Scooby Gang were her Knights of the Round Table. The school librarian, Rupert Giles, was also Buffy's watcher, appointed to this post by the Council (a British-based organisation which oversaw the Slayer's duties) and in time he became her Merlin and his library their Camelot.

And woven within this tapestry of timing, writing, broadcasting and TV trendsetting, there was Spike, the sarcastic vampire and sometime gentle poet, with devilish good looks and serious street cred, the unexpected darling of the fans and runaway ratings-winner for the series.

But what did this all have to do with an unknown Autist, a world away from Joss Whedon and the WB Television Network?

At the time, not a lot.

It takes many tales to make up a legend, though, and Spike had a demonic girlfriend called Drusilla. Dru was beautiful, blue-eyed, brunette and bonkers. She dressed in what's been described as "*a cross between a Victorian period look and the Kate Moss heroin chic fashion look*" which made her the Nancy Spungen to Spike's platinum-blond Sid Vicious. She spoke in rhyme and foresaw the future. Perhaps she foresaw mine, and if that was the first time she called to me in her wise and quiet way, then I was the fool who did not hear. I was a long way from Los Angeles, but watching *Buffy* after a tiring shift was becoming a pleasant habit and in view of the disappointments I'd known the Scoobies' 'All for One and One for All' camaraderie struck a chord. But nothing more than that.

Yet still it seemed she called, and one evening deep in the winter of 2005, Drusilla the vampire appeared in an episode of

Buffy and lit up the screen, displaying the kind of queenly grace and dark allure no man could fail to notice.

Great acting by a great actress and Juliet Landau, I remembered, was her name.

6

Sullen xenophobia

No, you never can tell how things will turn out. I'd let my flat in Glasgow to a tenant while I pursued my hopeless dream elsewhere. After nearly a year at the Welcome Break, I was weary if not unhappy, wondering if toilets and bins were the shape of things to come, when my tenant announced he was leaving.

So it was time for me to make a decision. Stay amidst the toilets but enjoy the rural idyll with another tenant bankrolling me, or go back to Glasgow and keep on trying to live an independent life.

I wasn't exactly champing at the bit to go back to the dear green place. The city had its kind and welcoming people, and many of them, but I wasn't exactly missing a town where there was never very much work, where poverty kept seeping through the cracks in the thin façade of prosperity, where the embers of sectarianism smouldered just beneath the leafy surface and, as I was about to find out, where there were a few too many arrogantly ignorant, racist loudmouths who made Ena Sharples and Jade Goody look like amateurs.

These were the sort of people who were kind only to those who were exactly like them, and treated anyone who was not with a sullen xenophobia bordering on sociopathy.

Lynsey Hanley, a writer who grew up on a council estate, once said: *"its people were warm towards others who looked and acted exactly like them, but unforgiving, going on vicious, with anyone who didn't."*

Such people, unable to get jobs elsewhere, were often soaked up by Scotland's large and flabby public sector, which tended to turn a blind eye to the behaviour of their staff as long as the work got done. So offices would turn into ghettos while managers talked sincerely of taking great strides towards equality, knowing they would be safe as long as no-one said or did anything to shake the status quo.

My family had seen this all before. Returning to Scotland in the 1970s and unwisely going to work in the public sector, my father found himself the subject of vicious backstabbing by officials with chips on their shoulders because he was the only one of them who had a degree, because he spoke (in their view) with an English accent, and because he did not just knuckle under and take the abuse they felt they had the divine right to deliver.

The small town where we settled was no better. The locals did not like incomers, seemed to derive a vindictive pleasure from finding out anything to another's discredit, and had a 'council house' mentality – rent a council house (never, *ever* buy), work for the council and subsist on a council pension – and their views were fixed. They always voted Labour, everything was Margaret Thatcher's fault, and nobody ever spoke up.

That, I think, was the worst thing. The number of people who stood back while my father fought to keep his job and a roof over his family's head (we were in a tied house – no job, no house), who vowed they would speak up on his behalf, but who then backed down when he asked them to keep their word. My father's secretary, for example. The union representative was waiting eagerly in my father's office, but with half-an-hour to go she changed her mind and refused to say anything.

My parents had never before seen such vicious and venal behaviour.

As for myself, as well as staggering through secondary school with unknown and undiagnosed Asperger's, I saw with awful clarity the worst aspects of human nature. Perhaps my autism accentuated the clear perception with which I saw the depth of those people's worthlessness, but to this day, if anyone gives me their word, they had better keep it.

It would be easy to say that all Autists see things in black and white, whereas for neuro-typicals everything is in shades of grey, but it is not as simple as that. Although an Autist might be quicker to see the factual difference between right and wrong, it takes real guts for anyone to stand against the crowd. Autists can be just as cowardly as neuro-typicals, and I'd rather have someone who stood by my side in a tight spot than a fair-weather friend any day of the week.

I escaped from that awful little town in 1985, but the knowledge I gained there has never left me.

What I did not foresee was that, in 2006, I would learn it all over again.

7

In the ghetto

I found a part-time job filing for the Glasgow branch of a large public sector organisation. I informed my new employers in writing that I had Asperger Syndrome and attended a 45-minute meeting with an Occupational Health nurse where I explained everything I could to them about autism.

I should have checked more carefully with Jim Doherty of the NAS, who could have carried out an assessment of my new workplace. He would have probably taken one look at it, told me not to touch it with a ten-foot bargepole, and thus averted disaster, but it never occurred to me to do so. By that time, I had had nearly 20 years' work experience in a variety of places and had no particular reason to assume I was suddenly incapable of coping in a reasonably well-run office.

Unfortunately, I was not going to be working in a reasonably well-run office. I was going into a ghetto which was descending into anarchy. A director of the Yorkshire branch of the organisation once said that they had employed *"too many who are lazy, unproductive, obstinate, militant, aggressive at every turn and who couldn't secure a job anywhere outside the bloated public sector where mediocrity is too often shielded by weak and unprincipled HR policies."*

The Glasgow branch was no better. I learnt later that Occupational Health failed to pass the paperwork about autism to my new office, but even if it had been delivered it wouldn't have made any difference. Within weeks of my arrival I found that discipline had completely broken down. The team leader reminded me of Ernst Stavro Blofeld as portrayed by Donald Pleasence in *You Only Live Twice*. He hid in a corner (thankfully, he didn't sit stroking a Persian cat) and in answer to any question came the whiny comment:

"I'll get back to you..."

Guess what? He never did.

Worse, he sucked up to two trouble-making administrative officers. One was a self-confessed loudmouth, the other just hadn't confessed. 'Blofeld' allowed them to think they were in charge and that, when he left, they would go 'one rung up the ladder' and step into his shoes. There was that old, sickly smell of cosy arrangements and back-scratching again, a situation that might not have been quite so bad if the troublemakers were actually any good at managing or supervising. They weren't. They once spent 45 minutes trying to work out a tea rota, and they *failed*. It would be very easy to call them stupid, but neither of them ever stopped talking long enough to let their brains start working.

They seemed to think that orders were the start of a conversation – and their conversation was one long, unending moan about pay and conditions, all to the tune of the local commercial radio station which played the same songs over and over and over again.

I'll never forget one incisive comment about a new employment contract:

"I don't think that's fair!"

Bawled out long and loud, like an undisciplined infant in primary school.

As the organisation had no redundancy policy, those with permanent contracts were virtually unsackable. So the moaning troublemakers had jobs for life in an area of high unemployment, as well as the chance to contribute to one of the UK's last gold-plated pension schemes and retire at 60. They may well have come from deprived areas and broken homes, but they had had chances too, and as I listened to the non-stop flow of spiteful drivel any sympathy I might have had for them began to dry up.

I wasn't the only one who had to listen to them. I had a fellow filer. He was an intelligent, well-spoken black man from Africa, but the loudmouths either talked over him, talked down to him or ignored him. We both usually tried to work in the basement to get away from them and one day in private, he begged me to tell him why they could never shut up.

"They've yakked all their lives," I said soberly. "They've yakked in the back of class, yakked at the back of the dole queue and yakked in the backrooms of pubs. And no one has ever told them to stop."

The office filing system was overloaded and failing. As usual, the management had blindly put their faith and at least £10 billion pounds of taxpayers' money into yet another grandiose IT project which, due to the near-impossibility of retrospectively converting millions of paper records, would not be ready until 2016 and, even if it worked, would by then already be obsolete.

Or so an IT technician had told me on the quiet.

It was anarchy, set to the grinding beat of the radio's drum.

I couldn't just walk out. There were no other jobs to go to.

I complained to more senior managers several times. They did absolutely nothing. One morning I (reluctantly) walked in and nodded to my black friend.

I remember he just looked back at me, his eyes empty, and said he felt like walking out, just leaving.

Perhaps I am racist, for I was beginning to prefer the black workers I met to the white moaners I had to endure. Every morning when I walked in, I passed a black cleaning lady who gave me a shining smile. My black friend invited me to his home, shared his food with me and called me his brother.

I also began to learn the hard way why Autists often needed workplaces to be adapted for them. People with autism have weak central coherence: we can be hypersensitive to light and sound, and we do not cope well with confined spaces. Unlike my black friend, I couldn't filter out the gossip and radio noise around me. After a while my defences were shredded and the overcrowded office environment became torture.

A BBC article about the use of music in torture explained that:

> *"The idea is to have no variation: the same sounds over and over again ... Deprivation of normal sensory stimulation and lack of control over one's environment is a disempowerment that eventually dehumanises people."*

That was *exactly* how it felt. Commercial radio stations have a very repetitive playlist (ie the same sounds over and over again) and I was nearer to the radio than the other staff.

When I complained about the noise, they deliberately turned it up. Like nasty little children, they tortured me, and I think they enjoyed it.

After nine months of this, I went back to Occupational Health. I was a complete nervous wreck and my right hand would not stop shaking.

They put me on sick leave, which might have seemed a blessing, but in fact it turned out to be a curse.

8

Looking into the abyss

Autists hate being kept hanging: we need routine and certainties. Leaving us in limbo is one of the worst things others can do to us.

I was on sick leave for nearly six months. To this day, I have no doubt it was another symptom of the laissez-faire culture of the organisation, summed-up as follows:

Leave the problem alone and perhaps it will go away!

Or, more precisely:

Perhaps the problem will have a convenient nervous breakdown so we can wash our hands of him and carry on smugly in our own sweet way!

I was handed over to a senior therapist for 'care', but I will never forget the way he tried to make excuses for the troublemakers' behaviour:

"They've got poor educational qualifications," he said. "They don't know any better."

So there are special rules for them, then, are there? I thought. *They're allowed to act like a bunch of overgrown spiteful children all day long because of their backgrounds?*

No, that's not all of it. You're just making excuses because you haven't got the guts to stand up to them. You know what they're like. You know what they do, but so long as the work gets done you just lie back and let them get away with it.

And if anyone sticks his head up and complains, you shoot the messenger and plead self-defence.

You bunch of utter cowards.

Nonsense like this came and went. Mostly it came, and usually it hung around. Human Resources admitted it had completely failed to deal with an autistic employee. Jim Doherty of the NAS took up my case with guts and honour. By so doing, he helped me regain some faith in human nature, but for most of the time I had to sit at home, sweat and wait, not knowing what would happen next or when.

The strain began to build. I applied for other jobs, I cared for my mother (my father had died in 1999 and I'd taken charge of her administrative affairs) and I tried to let the ringing in my head from the radio as well as the shaking in my hand go away.

But my hand would not stop shaking, for the torture had not stopped. As long as my future was uncertain, the stress went right on rubbing my nerves, stretching my fragile composure as tight as skin on a drum.

I began to snap and swear, my mouth was permanently dry and at times I felt I was hyperventilating. A neuro-typical might have been able to kid himself that everything would turn out all right, but I did not have that ability to delude myself. It was a summer morning in the family home when something began to tear in my mind. There was stillness in the air as I quietly looked into the abyss.

In the nearest thing to an act of desperation I have ever known, I phoned Jim Doherty. I didn't get him right there and then, but I think that taking some action, contacting another human being and, however clumsily I did so, blurting out that I was in trouble, helped me to avoid a breakdown.

Perhaps my articulacy has always been my greatest strength. The strong and silent types are often the ones who crack. Those who can put a voice to their fears and admit their flaws may just avoid falling apart like a scattered deck of cards.

I took a breath, and then another, feeling the panic begin to fade away. I was not all right. I was very far from all right, but I was in control of myself – and the moment had passed. The side-effects would last for years, but I was still on my feet and I had survived.

9

Cheating fate

Fighters look you in the eye but fellow workers, of the kind I had encountered, stab you in the back, and if you are old, frail, vulnerable, disabled or just plain different that's an added bonus. It's a chink in your armour they can exploit.

Occupational Health tried to put me back in the workplace. The troublemakers immediately blackmailed the management by saying, 'if James comes back, we'll go off sick.'

In a Hollywood film, a principled manager often played by the likes of Spencer Tracy or Gregory Peck would have said, "go, then."

But Glasgow was not Hollywood, so the management allowed themselves to be blackmailed and blocked me from returning. The six-month limit of my sick leave was fast approaching – and with it, the sack.

Either God or the luck of the Devil was with me, though, and an autism-suitable post doing data entry came up at the last moment. I cheated fate, the organisation was unable to wash its hands of me, and I was placed in a proper office with decent people who knew how to behave.

But my hand still shook, and I was angry that the organisation seemed to have learnt no lessons from the debacle and the troublemakers had got away scot-free.

I saw my doctor about my hand, and talked to him about it.

"It depends on you," he said. "Most people would try to put the matter behind them."

"I'm not most people," I said.

I submitted a formal grievance. The organisation kept me waiting for six months in order to ensure I could not take them to an employment tribunal, then tried to say the whole mess had been my fault.

I always remember that, in their written reply, they failed even to spell the word Asperger correctly. That, almost more than anything else, showed me how little they cared about or understood anyone even slightly unlike them.

Jim Doherty is the saintliest of men, but the day he read the organisation's reply was the closest I ever saw him come to anger.

"They've tried to blame you for everything," he said.

There was no happy Hollywood ending. Jim and I fought on and eventually fought them to a draw.

And what of my black friend? He applied for job after job to get away from that ghetto which he hated as much as I did, and finally he got his wish. Unfortunately, there are things one should beware wishing for. His new office was worse than the old one. The bigots banded together against him and after five months he resigned, even though he had no job or benefit to go to.

I stay in touch with him to this day, and not long ago he said to me:

"I have seen corruption, violence and injustice in Africa, but neither my wife nor myself had ever witnessed such disgusting and xenophobic behaviour until I came to work in Glasgow."

10

Punchy

In the fourteenth round of the Thrilla in Manila, Muhammad Ali should have knocked Joe Frazier down six times, but Frazier's sheer willpower kept him on his feet.

Autists have a fragile side: too much information can overload us too easily – but we do also have willpower. Six times and more, the organisation tried to bludgeon me to my knees and six times and more I'd staggered and buckled and covered up against their onslaught and stayed on my feet.

After six months' sick leave, I started data entry work in August 2007. I was out of shape, half a stone overweight and half dead with stress and fatigue. The radio noise, loudmouthed gossip, uncertainty, injustice and endless waiting and hanging had hit me as hard as any punch Frazier ever received from Ali.

My hand still quivered and my 'processor' was working even more slowly than usual (if that was possible). At the time, I honestly thought I had suffered permanent damage and would remain as I had become – even more slow-thinking and less able to cope with change.

In a word, punchy.

Well, at least I wasn't slurring my words, and if I had been able to recondition myself once at the Welcome Break, perhaps I could do so again. Mind you, I felt more like I needed a full-on resurrection.

I began re-establishing my routines. I made myself walk home from work to shed the excess weight. Every evening I cleaned one part of my flat, and after that I would turn to my bookshelves and bring down my pride and joy, my brand-new *Buffy the Vampire Slayer* DVD boxset.

Joss Whedon once said he'd "rather have a show that a

hundred people *need* to see than a thousand *like* to see," and for most of 2008 I needed to see his show.

It wasn't escapism. I had seen too much of people's bad sides. It was a relief to see the better side of human nature depicted, and *Buffy* could make even an Autist empathise with its characters.

For most of 2008, I watched an episode every night and, very slowly, I found myself beginning to take an interest in Spike's girlfriend, Drusilla.

There is a difference between observing and obsessing, and while Autists can be obsessive, it is a natural trait of ours. Taking a focused interest in one subject for a long time may be a sign of mental disorder in a neuro-typical, but it is quite normal for an Autist – as long as the Autist is high functioning, socially experienced and mature enough to know how far to go.

So how did I find the road which would lead me to that sunlit city, Los Angeles?

I'm not even sure myself.

There is an old film called *Stalag 17* starring William Holden and set in a World War II German POW camp. Every time an escape is attempted, someone tips off the Germans and Holden is suspected of being the traitor. He is beaten up, ostracised and left alone in the prisoners' dormitory.

He doesn't rant, he doesn't curse, he doesn't obsess. He just lies on a bench and looks.

And finally he sees.

Every time an escape attempt had been imminent, someone tied up a light fitting's cable in a distinctive way, alerting the Germans.

The most important things in life are not easily seen at first glance.

Like Holden, I didn't rant, I didn't curse and I didn't obsess. I just sat there, like a battered boxer after a brutal fight.

I sat there and slowly I began to see Drusilla. Like her favourite flower, she only bloomed at night, in forgotten corners or just out of sight; the tragic Ophelia to Buffy's loudmouthed Hamlet, otherwise known as Spike.

Like Spike, Dru was indeed a killer. But in the same way that he was a lovelorn poet at heart, she was also a gentle girl: even as a demon and a murderess, she was still sweeter and kinder at heart than the money-grubbing mediocrities to whom I had so recently been exposed.

I did not really realise it at the time, but beneath the monster's mantle, I began to see the vulnerable girl, and she began to strike a chord.

The first episodes in which I noticed Drusilla were *Fool For Love* and *Crush*, in which she appeared first in flashback sequences depicting Spike's past life, then as a rather lonely ex-girlfriend in the present day, trying to win Spike back, and failing.

Buffy and Angel had the first televisual romance between a human and a vampire, which inspired films and TV series like the *Twilight* saga and *True Blood* to explore the themes of human/demon relationships and the integration of the undead into human society. But Spike and Dru were the first vampires to be depicted as something more than one-dimensional bad guys and gals, basically just there to be staked by Buffy to the accompaniment of wry and trendy quips like "we haven't been properly introduced, I'm Buffy, and you're history," or "All *right*, I get it. You're evil. Do we have to chat about it all day?"

Unlike the tortured, brooding Angel, Spike and Dru were ostensibly straightforward classic vampires of the old school – soulless killers who hated the sun and the Scoobies. However they were also a couple who loved and cared for each other and showed emotional vulnerability, thus enabling Whedon's viewers to relate to them as beings, if not *human* beings. The first true vampire/vampire romance on television, which helped pave the way for the complex social questions posed more recently by *True Blood*. What if, instead of just being befanged baddies there to be killed, Spike and Dru got US citizenship, moved in next door to you and tried to be good neighbours?

For me, though, academic study of vampires as depicted by the entertainment media was still in the future. Perhaps the first moment I began to care for Drusilla was in *Crush*. Spike rejected her for Buffy and physically dumped her, throwing her to the floor of his crypt and turning away from her to aid Buffy, supposedly their mortal enemy.

Because our brains have a bias towards logic, Autists are not big on empathy and have difficulty relating to others. I sat through *The English Patient* and felt nothing, and there were only two actresses in the world who could make me react emotionally – Julia Roberts and Jolene Blalock (T'Pol on *Star Trek: Enterprise*). Now there was Juliet Landau.

So when Drusilla slowly picked herself up and looked at Spike, realising she had lost him and was alone in the world, I began to see her – and she began to get to me.

•

11

Behind the monster's mantle

William Holden lay on a bench and looked. James Christie sat at a desk, not yet seeing; and Juliet Landau, unknowing, lived her life in Hollywood.

I was in an office identical to the one I had tried to escape by going to the cataloguing agency, the employment I had fought so long and so hard to hold on to was virtually meaningless. Basic data entry which did not stretch even my crippled information-processing capabilities. My prospects were nil and I remained part of an organisation whose heart was dark as Joseph Conrad's Congo.

Although I seemed stuck in the shadowlands of lost hope and middle age, there were little chinks of light. The people with whom I was now working were fine and decent, I was hanging in redeployment limbo and under no pressure to perform, and I had internet access. The door to the sunlit city on the hill.

And in my mind, Drusilla was beginning to come to life.

Forget the ruin of your life, I thought. *Forget the fact you're locked in career jail as surely as William Holden was locked in that POW camp. Forget that the neurons in your brain are sparking as irregularly as electronic linkages in a fuse box after it's been hit by a sledgehammer. Just look. Look for tales of the gentle girl behind the monster's face.*

So, in between tasks and the slow tick of the long day's clock, I searched out Drusilla.

Fan-fiction – stories illegally written about films and TV shows by the fans – has been around for as long as moving pictures themselves, and with the rise of the internet such stories have become far more freely available to the public via websites such as FanFiction.Net. The standard of writing is, to put it tactfully, variable. The best authors could cut it professionally, the worst are ungrammatical, self-indulgent and inept. However, despite such flaws fan-fiction provides a wonderful forum for self-expression. Authors write for the love of their favourite characters and free from most of the cut-throat competition of the publishing industry.

Because the characters of whom you write are not your own there is a certain sense, as a fan-fiction writer, that you are defying the system. All stories must be preceded by a disclaimer stating that copyright does not belong to the author and that s/he will derive no profit from the tale. This disclaimer does not protect the author from prosecution and is mainly a statement of the author's position, as well as a sentence essentially begging the copyright holders (20th Century Fox, Warner Brothers etc.) not to sue him or her. They can still do so if they wish, but with millions of fan-fiction stories in circulation it would probably not be cost-effective.

So fan-fiction and free expression survives.

Years earlier, a fan-fiction writer called Jason Thompson had created a Drusilla website which specialised in stories about Dru and Xander, a member of Buffy's Scooby gang. Except for one hard and realistic piece, where Dru murders Xander for putting her under a love spell, the stories all depicted Dru showing a soft spot for Xander, calling him 'kitten' and falling in love with him.

Xander – full name Alexander LaVelle Harris and portrayed by Nicholas Brendon – is a member of Buffy's Scooby gang and the only character to possess no special powers or abilities. Xander was virtually estranged from his dysfunctional parents and notably immature at first although he grew up markedly over the course of *Buffy's* seven seasons, gaining employment as a carpenter and eventually being recognised as one of Buffy's truest friends. His honest bravery (shown by his willingness to take on supernatural foes without any special powers of his own, simply because it was the right thing to do) and his unswerving loyalty to Buffy made him something of a chivalric character in the mould of Sir Thomas Malory's knights – Buffy's 'white knight,' as Angelus once sneered. However, these high cultural characteristics were ably counterpointed by Joss Whedon's scripting, which avoided too much highbrow noble elegy by making Xander the king of pop culture with a nice line in self-deprecating humour. An Everyman to whom the average working Joe could relate, as well as a Galahad for the modern day with a lopsided grin and a ready quip, as vulnerable in his way as Drusilla was in hers.

A neuro-typical could probably get the hang of Xander's character traits in a second, but for me the effort it took to understand the emotions of another was akin to moving blocks of masonry into place and I could never be entirely sure I'd got it right.

Paradoxically, although I had come to understand the importance of communicating and socialising, I struggled to do so because the 'caring software' in my brain simply didn't function well enough to let me. Unable to trust my emotional instincts and having to push my substandard 'caring software' to its limits in order to empathise, I had little sympathy (or empathy!) for neuro-typicals who, despite being equipped with fully functional emotional software, selfishly hurt their partners, bailing out of relationships with pathetic excuses like:

"I'm just not ready for a relationship right now..."

"I'm afraid of commitment..."

And my all-time favourite, usually accompanied by a shifty look and much hand-wringing:

"It's complicated..."

The funny thing, though, was that while I struggled to comprehend Xander, I did feel an easy, natural empathy for Dru, although I didn't really understand why.

I suspect I have about 10-20 percent of a neuro-typical's natural empathy. It's a bit like a radio signal. NTs get crystal-clear FM reception, Autists hear an indistinct message, fading in and out through washes of static and sometimes disappearing altogether.

Julia Roberts' emotional radio signal must be extraordinarily strong. It is a natural characteristic which cannot be learned, and one reason she is an A-list movie star. Jolene Blalock has the same ability, and I always knew what was going through her mind when she looked at Captain Archer...

Then there was Dru. And as I read more Dru/Xander fan-fiction and reran the scene in *Crush* where she got dumped, I began to empathise more with the sweet girl behind the monster's face.

But was my empathy for Drusilla the character, for Juliet Landau who portrayed her, or for both of them?

Now *that* was complicated.

12

The Great Scottish Novel

Have you ever met one of those people who always end up standing in the kitchen at parties? The geeky weirdo with a patched and scruffy beard, whose glasses date from 1973, who (if you are particularly unlucky) will fix you with an unnervingly intense stare, deliver a lecture about the homoerotic subtext in *Top Gun* and, before he vanishes into the night, mutter something about writing The Great Scottish, English or American Novel.

I am more than a little relieved to say I'm clean-shaven, my glasses are of a later vintage than 1973 and I have no particular knowledge of *Top Gun's* homoeroticism, but in one respect I have to admit I am a geek. I spent 15 years trying to write The Great Scottish Novel.

Now do you believe Autists are single-minded with a narrow range of interests?

I used to manacle myself to my old Canon word processor all night long, manically drafting and redrafting in a doomed attempt to tie together disparate elements of theme and plot. I forgot to seek out inebriated women and they forgot to look for me. On one occasion, after spending months inside my tenement flat surrounded by books on Celtic history, I took a night off, walked round Glasgow city centre, and marvelled at all the new buildings that seemed miraculously to have appeared from nowhere.

And all my relentless labour came to naught. The book did not work. Thousands of hours of blood, sweat and misery had all been for nothing. I had always known how great the odds were against me, and although it was not much consolation at the time, the doomed project had given me a prodigious amount of practice and fully developed my writing ability.

According to the article *How To Be A Genius* in the *New Scientist* of September 16 2006, although some people are indeed born with greater genetic gifts than others *"some critical things line up so that a person of good intelligence can put in the sustained, focused effort it takes to achieve extraordinary mastery."* Just having great talent or intelligence on its own was not enough, it seemed. That talent had to be built, honed and painstakingly sculpted. There also seemed to be a ten-year rule: *"it seems you have to put in at least a decade of focused work to master something and bring greatness within reach."*

What happened to the brain as a result of this work? The article seemed to have the answer:

"Eric Kandel of Columbia University in New York, who won a Nobel prize in 2000 for discovering much of the neural basis of memory and learning, has shown that both the number and strength of the nerve connections associated with a memory or skill increase in proportion to how often and how emphatically the lesson is repeated. So focused study and practice literally build the neural networks of expertise."

I read that article just after I'd finished the final draft of my Great Scottish Novel and a little while before its final rejection. I was pleased in some ways, dejected in others. Although my brain was autistic I'd put in, not ten, but *15* years of work to bring the neural networks of my verbal IQ (my articulacy and writing ability) up to par. Despite the deficiencies in my performance IQ, my 'Asperger focus' had actually given me an advantage, helping me to concentrate on developing a particular skill more easily than a multi-tasking neuro-typical might.

I imagined the way those neural networks must actually have grown and thickened, helping the sparks of inspiration flow more easily. Whereas a talented but unpractised writer might only have the equivalent of low voltage domestic wiring in his brain, I now had heavy duty commercial cabling.

However, I was not yet quite at my peak. It had not been easy for me to develop the personalities of the characters in my Great Scottish Novel, or to chart their social interactions. Nor did I really care about them. If the plot had demanded it, I would cheerfully have thrown them screaming into a volcanic crater full of white hot magma.

So, rather like a vampire in its prime, the creative writing machine in my mind was ready to roll but lacked a soul. That indefinable element which separates the moderately good from the great. Then along came Drusilla. Not exactly the kind of girl you'd expect to fall in love with.

But I did.

13

A door into summer

I didn't see her clearly at first, and I scarcely thought of Juliet Landau, the actress who played her, but perhaps there is a fate that shapes our ends or a synchronicity which brings our lives together, if only we can look and see.

I read Dru and Xander fan-fiction at work and at home, slowly getting an impression of the lost girl locked within the demon, clothing her image in flesh like a walking hologram I could summon at will. I would always see her as she was in Season Two of *Buffy*, clad in harlot's red with long and curly hair.

Temple Grandin, the most famous Autist in America and a professor at Colorado State University, once said "I think in pictures." Many Autists can do the same, and I now think that what at first felt slightly disconcerting was, in autistic terms, quite normal. I would think about Drusilla – so naturally I could see her, and I got to like having her around.

A fan-fiction writer with the web pseudonym Mahaliem wrote a superb trilogy of tales about Dru and Xander which perfectly caught her vulnerability. A prolific author called Meltha crafted poignant and sometimes comic pieces about the lost girl and created Drusilla's section of the *Buffy* Writers' Guild website, known as *Charm School, version: Lessons in Etiquette*. A strange title which perhaps refers to the oddly charming way Dru sometimes behaved and the bloody lessons she would deliver if someone breached her warped, but still Victorian, ideals of etiquette. Or merely if she was hungry.

It is one of the oddities of the internet era: I would come to know and respect Meltha greatly without ever finding out who he or she was, but my favourite Dru and Xander story was *Xander's Secret*, an unfinished piece of fan-fiction written by Zillagirl in 2007.

In *Xander's Secret*, Xander meets Drusilla in London six months after the town of Sunnydale collapsed into a crater at the end of the climactic battle in *Chosen* (the last episode of *Buffy*), an event which came to be known as the Fall of Sunnydale. Xander starts going to afternoon tea at Dru's flat and begins to fall in love with her:

> *"Druse, no offense, but I don't think I'd like having rotten cream. Okay? How 'bout just plain old whipp—" Xander stopped and spun in horror at the soft snarl he heard emanating from Drusilla.*
>
> *"I do NOT make rotten food!" She spat at him angrily. How dare he say such a thing to her? And she had thought they were friends. Ohhhhh! Things like that made her so angry.*
>
> *Xander looked on in shock, his horror subsiding somewhat, as her face shifted back and forth from human to demon and back again. He came to realize, somewhat slowly, that she wasn't going all evil and homicidal on him. She was angry... angry and hurt. He felt a slow burn of shame wash all over him. He'd hurt her feelings. Ever since he knew her, he was always amazed at how sensitive she was. How easily she was hurt.*

Drusilla herself, originally a pure, sweet and chaste Catholic girl born in the London of 1840 before being driven insane and turned into a vampire was, according to essays on the *Charm School* website, particularly difficult to portray accurately. She was mentally ill, traumatised, seemingly immature, dependent yet devious, psychic, away with the fairies and in a world of her own most of the time, strangely innocent yet rather promiscuous, prone to speaking in rhyme, deeply vulnerable but extremely dangerous and both a modern-day Ophelia and an example of heroin-chic.

So Drusilla would appear in fan-fiction stories as either completely goopy, totally randy, pathetically needy or even utterly stoned. Very few writers could convey the shifting hues of the multicoloured dreamcoat of conflicting characteristics which made up Dru. Relatively few tried, preferring to concentrate on Spike, Buffy and Angel, and even fewer tried to write stories about Dru and Xander.

But for me and my damaged brain, now subconsciously uploading and analysing Drusilla's complex set of personality traits, reading about her was like opening a door into summer. By 2008, I had spent three years seeing the worst sides of human nature close-up. Even though Drusilla had been turned into a psychotic, murderous demon with a penchant for the innocent blood of children, there was a sweet side to her which was still more pleasant than some of the real-life people I'd met.

Drusilla the soulless vampire, kinder at heart than so-called caring humans.

Over the course of 2008, the story which would become *Drusilla's Roses* began to assemble itself in my head as my neural networks painstakingly restored themselves. I didn't know this was happening, still assuming I was punchy and probably going to stay that way. Nor did I think to question why I suddenly seemed to be feeling such empathy for a fictional character. Looking back now, after all the surreal and wondrous events which have since come to pass, I can only assume that some strange synchronicity was indeed at work.

Drusilla seemed to be the only creature, real or imagined, who could touch my damaged soul and bring me back to the way I was; and it seemed that with my writing skills, I was the one chosen to develop her character.

Quite unaware of this tapestry being woven around me, I grew more and more comfortable with the strange vampire girl now alive in my mind and, when I wished to see her, gliding shyly around my flat.

I resolved to try and answer two questions which the writers of *Buffy the Vampire Slayer* had left unresolved:

- At the end of the last *Buffy* episode, *Chosen*, the Scoobies stand by the ruins of Sunnydale and asked each other the question, "what do we do now?" Although Joss Whedon & Co. had gone on to write the comic book series *Buffy*

Season 8, the action only began some months after the Fall of Sunnydale. No fan-fiction or professional writer had ever quite managed to answer the Scoobies' question: What had happened *just after* the closing credits of *Chosen*?

- Whatever happened to Drusilla? Even the Internet Movie Database had asked that very question. Except for flashbacks, she had made no appearance in *Buffy* since Season Five and although she, together with Angel, Spike and Darla, was a member of the villainous vampire family nicknamed the Fanged Four, she, unlike the others, had not been redeemed from evil. She was just out there somewhere, lost and alone, with no-one to bring her home.

Was it destiny that brought two lives together?

I only know this:

In December 2008, as the shape and form of *Drusilla's Roses* began to coalesce in the mind of a man in a flat in Partick, a woman flew into Glasgow for a comics convention at Braehead Shopping Centre.

And neither James Christie nor Juliet Landau knew that, seven weeks before *Roses* began, they were less than two miles apart, or that the other was there.

14

Opening the Pukka pad

There are those who say there is no fate but what we make ourselves. Others believe our destiny is predetermined, that although we may believe we have free will, we can only march to the beat of another's drum.

Perhaps our only choice is whether or not to march. To retrieve and shoulder that old and creaking harness from the dusty leather chest to which it was consigned long ago. To wear the old armour no longer seen in the modern day. To feel the song within us once more, as it was when we were young.

I did not then hear Drusilla's song, but perhaps she sang to both of us in those early days. First to Juliet Landau, who had just begun to write a two-part Drusilla story for IDW Publishing's *Angel* comic book series, and then to me.

Miss Landau later said she was *"drawn into Dru's rich, dark world"*, and so was I. In fact, I was positively *yanked*. The 08.12 to Mallaig, sitting at one end of the West Highland Railway in Glasgow's Queen Street Station, might have seemed a long way from Los Angeles, but both places saw Drusilla's rebirth and both were as real as real could be.

It was January 31 2009. I was going up to the West Highland town of Glenfinnan for the annual general meeting of the *Friends of Glenfinnan Station Museum*. For no particularly well-thought-out reason, I'd bought a green Pukka Pad jotter with me to make notes and perhaps to do some writing...

I opened the jotter, put pen to paper, and Dru grabbed me by the throat.

I've known bad writers and worse film-makers who reach for a cliché at every turn, but real life can often put fiction to shame. If I must label my experience a thunderclap high above the hills which let vitality and creativity run like fire through my veins, if I must say my pen began to shoot across the page as if it had a mind of its own, that I completely ignored the views of Loch Long, Ben Lomond and Rannoch Moor, nearly forgot to get off the train at Glenfinnan and wandered through the meeting half-aware, thinking only of getting back on the train to Glasgow afterwards and writing some more, then that is what I shall do, and without apology, for that is what really happened that day. I began to move away from the drab and vicious life I had known, to open the door into what would become a glimpse of heaven at Sunset.

And if that is cliché, I only wish I could live every day of my life that way.

15

An odd couple

From *Drusilla's Roses:*

> *So what do you do once you've saved the world?* Xander Harris thought to himself. *What follows the end of days, except more and more empty days, all winding along a slow, sad road towards oblivion. All observed in flat monochrome by the one-eyed man...*

As I wrote those first words somewhere between Sighthill and Springburn on the West Highland Railway, *something* happened, and it happened with frightening intensity.

Imagine a World War Two B-17 heavy bomber standing dusty and forgotten in an old USAF hangar. Patched, shot up and past its best. Imagine, then, its four Cyclone radial engines coughing into life and building up horsepower as the tyres strain against the chocks.

The fuselage seems to subtly ripple as the song of power spreads through the airframe. The wiring hums with electric vitality and the instruments softly glow. The aircraft, once a mute and lifeless hulk, is now vigorous and healthy. Then, with fine and graceful precision, the pilot opens the throttles.

At the time, I didn't really ask myself why my writing ability was spinning back into life with such disarming suddenness, or why I had begun to care so passionately and viscerally for Dru. My empathy never extended to the other characters in *Buffy* and with apologies to Michelle Trachtenberg – who played Buffy's sister, Dawn Summers, in *Buffy* seasons five to seven – I would have cheerfully deleted Dawn from *Roses* if canon (the official history of the fictional *Buffy* universe or 'Buffyverse') had not forbidden it. Dawn had been in the closing scene of *Chosen*. She would undoubtedly have gone with the others to Candlewood

My vampire flatmate

Drive where *Roses* commenced only a week or two later. Nor would Buffy have failed to notice the sudden disappearance of her sister, whom she loved and protected with a passion, so I was stuck with her.

I'm not really surprised I didn't spend time trying to divine the roots of my literary renaissance. If you find yourself unexpectedly flying a B-17 at 20,000 feet, what are you going to do? Read a book on aviation theory or grab the joystick, trim the throttles and try to keep the aircraft straight and level?

Not only that, I was *enjoying* writing about Dru and having her around. Sometimes homicidal but always sweet. We were an odd couple. The damaged, disabled man and his deranged flatmate. But she was my good companion in the wee small hours, when there was naught else in the world but she and I and *Roses*.

Juliet Landau had already been drawn back into Drusilla's world.

Now I was there too.

16

Drusilla's Roses

Drusilla's Roses was written between the end of January and the first week of April 2009 in what I can only call an explosion of creativity. I didn't plan out my chapters. I hadn't worked out my plot, and I didn't know what I was doing.

In psychological terms, I have heard that as well as an intelligence quotient (IQ), people have something called an emotional quotient (EQ). This is an estimated measure of emotional intelligence. While I am neither a psychologist nor a psychiatrist, it certainly felt to me like my EQ (not all that high to begin with) had been beaten to a pulp by my bruising experience with the organisation.

Presumably, my shredded EQ had been trying to find a way to regenerate itself and the very moment I began to write Roses, it locked onto Buffy's characters, plots and themes with a vengeance and would not let go.

Most of all, it locked onto Drusilla.

This was not a subtle or delicate experience. It felt as if once I had been blind but now I could see. My emotional intelligence came back to life and, rather than simply returning to its former level, it shot through the roof. This happened in a matter of seconds. Suddenly the not terribly empathic Asperger was feeling the whole gamut of human emotions in the raw. In Buffy terms, it was as if I'd had my soul restored. I felt giddy, elated.

I stayed that way for two months, and the plot, themes and characterisation came together as if by magic.

And Drusilla was alive in my mind. It was as if, like some faery sprite with unfinished business, she had been wandering the world, lost and looking for a writer who could resurrect her.

Now she had found me, taken up residence in my flat like a large dormouse, and like the writer's muse of myth, was inspiring me to the greatest sustained burst of creativity I'd ever known.

In the end, *Drusilla's Roses* ran to nearly 25,000 words, telling the tale of the traumatised Scoobies renting a house in Sylmar, Los Angeles, on a small street with a magical name:

The house on Candlewood Drive.

There Xander ran into Drusilla, traumatised herself and willing to renounce evil. They fell in love and she regained her soul – but there was a little twist at the end.

There is a fine line between creativity and obsession, between fantasy and delusion. I have a theory that autistic brains may be better able than those of NTs to handle the ups and downs of the creative impulse. One of autism's few universal symptoms is a tendency to be artistic and creative. It is possible that the design of the autistic brain's wiring makes it more able than the mind of a neuro-typical to accommodate that vital spark which drives the artist to perform. Unable to control their demons, some NT writers smoke, drink or take drugs to excess while quite a few artists seem susceptible to the highs and lows of bipolar disorder. I once heard that after writing *In Cold Blood*, the writer Truman Capote became a recluse, turned up drunk at talk shows and died in a pool of his own vomit.

Perhaps his demons did indeed drive him to destruction. My own demon, tall and raven-haired with big blue eyes, welcomed me home every evening with a gentle smile and made me happy.

Well aware of the reality of slow days and long nights writing in a Glasgow tenement, helped by a placid vampire flatmate always ready with hot chocolate in my favourite mug, I brought to life the untold tale of Drusilla the vampire. The seed of the story had gestated, grown, split and flowered in the right place, in the right hands and at the right time.

Xander's mouth dropped open. He willed himself to say the right thing and, as usual, failed.

"Hey, Dru. Out on the town for a bite to eat..?"

"I am standing on the chessboard with my white knight and I don't know my next move..."

"Dru," he said, "when this is all over, I'll stand you another cup of coffee at Starbucks..."

"Xander, just what is it with you and demon women..?"

Now, for the first time in many a long year, the vampire regarded the novice and found the strength to compare the gentle girl she had been with the monster she had become...

Dru and Xander lay together, the outline of their bodies etched in palest golden light. Like the statues of a knight with his lady one might see in an old English abbey...

Giles looked at Drusilla's roses in the moonlight, and watched Xander pace up and down...

"I don't want to talk about how I feel, Rupert," he said finally. "I don't want any wise words. I just don't want Dru hurt any more. She can be hurt so easily. She's just a little forgetful, you see. I mean, look at her roses. She's always saying everything she puts in the ground dies, but her roses are growing strong. She just needs someone to remind her to water them. That's all. Then she's all right..."

"Do they love each other, Giles?"

The watcher looked into the distance for a moment.

"Yes," he said. "They just don't know it..."

I hope my new family will not find me, Drusilla thought sadly to herself. Oh, my dearest enemies, I came to love you so! And my lovely boy, I wish I could have been your lady. I am sorry I must leave you, and I pray you will not have to see my face when it is over...

By early April, I was putting the finishing touches to *Roses* and, like Drusilla in the story, felt like I'd been cleansed with silver rain. Three months living on Candlewood Drive had reminded me of the better aspects of humanity.

I honed the final chapter, influenced by *Anna Karenina* and *To Kill a Mockingbird*. I'd looked to the classics for inspiration and found Tolstoy himself had been influenced by the spare, clear prose of childrens' books. Hemingway, too, had pioneered modern literature's more succinct prose style. I took a leaf out of their books in order to write my own.

April 8 2009.

I'd circulated two versions of the final chapter round the office to new colleagues who were so fine, decent and far removed from the guttersnipes of old that I could scarcely believe they worked for the same organisation and/or inhabited the same planet. If I was the chosen one, then they were my Scoobies, and we worked on *Roses'* last words together:

The new day was drawing near when he took her hand and led her from the church.

He walked with his lady to their home on Candlewood Drive. He greeted his friends, who were waiting at the door, and they invited her in.

She stumbled on the stairs as she walked up to her room. He helped her get into bed and watched her fall asleep. And for the first time in many years, she slept easily, knowing he would be there when she woke...

Then (as the protagonist of Stephen King's *Misery*, novelist Paul Sheldon, said) I "scrawled the most loved and hated phrase in the writer's vocabulary with a pen":

THE END

I clicked on Save and sat there contentedly for a few moments, but the clock ticked on and time did not stop.

Okay, I thought. *Now what?*

The rose of Candlewood Drive

17

The blunt instrument

The phone rang but I was lost and far away, my thoughts with the manuscript of *Drusilla's Roses* languishing in my hard drive and pictures of a real-life location I'd used in *Roses* revolving like a dream in the backwaters of my mind.

But here and now, the phone was ringing and the caller calling. It was Jim from the NAS.

"Hi there, James. We've got a problem."

"Like Houston? No, don't tell me, let me guess. You want to send me into space. First Asperger in the Moon..."

"Not quite that far. We need a representative with autism to meet several members of the Scottish Parliament at their Cadogan Street offices on Friday and our usual speaker can't make it."

"You want me to go along instead?"

"Yes," he said sweetly.

Great. Public speaking and social interaction. Just what we Autists are so good at.

On the other hand, I thought, Jim had heard me speak, I was much older and more experienced than most of his clients, and even if I couldn't perform very well in public I probably wouldn't have a panic attack.

"Okay, Jim. I've got no notes, no preparation and no idea what to say, but I owe the NAS a lot. I am happy to stand up and get my head beaten off on your behalf."

"Thanks, James. We really appreciate that."

Great.

And actually, it was.

Every Autist is different. What nobody, including me, knew was that I'd inherited my late father's public-speaking ability.

He had talked to heads of industry at major conferences in his days as a senior personnel manager with British Steel, and latterly to old ladies of the Women's Rural Institute in South Lanarkshire. He'd found out late in life that he had this talent and I, in middle age, was about to learn I'd inherited it lock, stock and barrel.

Jim had given me two days' warning so I did prepare myself as best I could, and I was accompanied by Carol Evans, then-director of the NAS in Scotland and Northern Ireland, but I didn't know what would happen when I actually started to speak.

A wry, confident and measured voice filled the room at Cadogan Street, and as the first faint tremors of nervousness faded briskly away I felt like an experienced rally driver moving through the gears and picking up speed.

If my writing ability could be likened to a B-17 high in flight at full power, my articulacy felt like a car with a plenitude of horsepower, factory fresh tyres tightly gripping the tarmac, guided easily with the lightest of touches.

Autist or not, my father's voice had been downloaded directly into my head and, perhaps rarely for one of us, I found I was actually good at public speaking.

After I'd clinically dissected various shortcomings in the Scottish public sector's treatment of the disabled, I chatted briefly with the Members of the Scottish Parliament.

"I'm the NAS' blunt instrument," I quipped at one point. "They bring me out for black ops."

I thought I'd overdone it for a moment and tried to take it back, but the Members liked it and it stuck. James Bond was M's 'blunt instrument'. Now I had been given my licence to kill for the NAS.

A joke, of course. I was a somewhat juvenile middle-aged man with a developmental disability, but somewhere in there a young man who'd once gone round the world was still to be found, and he was not quite ready to be claimed by that life of quiet desperation.

18

Keeper of the flame

What to do with *Drusilla's Roses*? I had written it and it was good, but the burst of creativity which had spawned it showed no sign of abating, I could not publish it (except on a fan-fiction website) and I was still on an emotional high, so what was I to do to bring myself down?

My neural networks were now repaired, I was no longer punchy and my hand shook no more. I was myself again, if a little fearful that like Charlie in *Flowers for Algernon* (the story of a simple-minded man whose IQ was artificially enhanced, only for him slowly and heartbreakingly to lose that intelligence bit by bit and revert to his former self) I might lose the emotional intelligence (EQ) I had gained.

I might even lose Drusilla, or at least the ability to write her. As Darla, a short, sarcastic blonde vampire who turned Angel into a vampire and became his murderous girlfriend before gaining a soul and an unborn baby by various unlikely plot devices, said of her child in an *Angel* episode:

> *"I won't be able to love her. I won't even be able to remember loving her!"*

A bit melodramatic, perhaps, but Autists and neuro-typicals do not think alike. While I knew perfectly well that Drusilla was fictional, she was alive and well in my mind. If my emotions dried up she'd have nowhere to go.

I didn't like the idea of that.

A simple, logical solution presented itself. As Leonard Nimoy stated in his second autobiography *I am Spock*, in terms of being faithful to a character, an actor is *"the keeper of the flame."*

The keeper of the flame

I was an Asperger, with the logical mind of a Vulcan. There was only one obvious choice to make.

Send *Drusilla's Roses* to Juliet Rose Landau.

I'd found the address of her production company on her website, so I bought a padded envelope, printed out a copy of *Roses* and prepared to send Dru home.

To Hollywood.

No tricks, but a hard-copy item was more likely to be read than an email attachment. Do that, then, and leave it to the fates. Write a covering letter, write out how you feel and get it out of your system. There's nothing else to be done. You can't publish. *Buffy* isn't being made any more. Just do it, dump *Roses* on a fan-fiction website, hope you don't get sued and say goodbye.

Put Dru in the care of her keeper and try to forget. Pour all your emotion and all your feeling into that letter. Let it go and never kid yourself that you'll ever know if she read it or what she thought.

I sent that package to Hollywood from a post office on Great Western Road and tried to walk away. Drusilla, however, stayed stubbornly alive in my mind, and even as the story headed out across the Atlantic, I did begin to wonder what would happen when it arrived in that faraway land of silver screens and olive groves.

What would she think when she opened the letter and read the first few lines? So many fans gushed all over the page. I had tried to be adult, polite and proper. An archaic phrase in the modern age, perhaps, but a fine beginning for a letter:

Dear Miss Landau.

Not too formal. Polite, not distant. Kind but business-like. That would do.

19

That quiet desperation

What would she think? I wondered despite myself. Then I reminded myself that I would never know. It was impossible.

The young man I'd been who'd gone round the world, perhaps he could have done it, could have walked with *Roses* through the desert to her door; but he'd lived in other days, 20 years and a millennium away. I wasn't him any more.

I was back to my old self, who was 44 and feeling it, and back at my old desk. Just like Reginald Perrin, I'd tried to change my life and ended up exactly where I'd started. At a desk identical to the one I'd left. Within shouting distance of the office I'd tried to escape.

Admittedly, I was more in touch with my nature and limitations; but despite this hard-won personal growth, destiny – like a satirical spinning wheel – had dumped me right back where I'd been before. Into that life of quiet desperation.

Though the song still dwelt within me.

Drusilla and the Scoobies were my companions for the long hours when I sat there entering data, and I dreamt of days of high adventure. Of heroes and their ladies. Of knights and dragons, and quests for swords and grails.

One fine afternoon in mid-May of 2009, I was browsing through the internet at work, using Google Maps to look at Candlewood Drive, drifting north along the California coast to Point Lobos, a State Reserve south of Carmel where I'd decided Drusilla would reach a turning point in her life. I found the official Point Lobos website and looked at the pictures.

The greatest meeting of land and water in the world, the artist Francis McComas had called it, and it was. A triangular headland of rocks burnished to a rich brown shade of leather by the sun, pine trees and secluded coves reaching out into the Pacific. Not so distant or secret as some places, but as far as a man might need to go in search of peace.

I saw the blue-green waters of one small cove, tinted cerulean and glowing like amethyst in soft light. I saw the waves washing onto the shore of gold and silver sand where Drusilla had walked at dawn, and knew I would never get there.

I'd known fear, stress and uncertainty, but only then did I feel Thoreau's quiet desperation, born of the realisation that I was trapped in middle age. That I would not go out again as I had gone before. That I would never see the house on Candlewood Drive or the beach at Point Lobos.

This time I was done, and there was no way home.

20

Purring lethally

Never say never, though, and if I really had been licensed to kill by the NAS, perhaps I should have said *Never Say Never Again*...

For, despite my best efforts to be a self-pitying jerk, I couldn't help wondering. *Roses* really had gone to California. Candlewood Drive and Point Lobos were no more than an air ticket away, and although Hollywood with its palm trees, stars and Oscars might seem like a mythic realm divorced from a cold and windy Byres Road with its pubs and charity shops, it was no heavenly Valhalla but an actual place. Surreal to the bystander on Byres Road. All too real to the struggling actor on the boulevard of broken dreams.

Then the phone rang again and, like an actor glad to hear from his agent, I picked up the receiver and took the call from Raemond Charles, the NAS Press & Publicity Officer.

There was media interest in a new film called *Adam* which had been chosen to close the Edinburgh Film Festival. *Rain Man* had been the first picture to deal with autism *per se* but *Adam* was the first movie to depict its milder variant, Asperger Syndrome. *Adam* was a love story about the ups and downs of a relationship between an Asperger and a neuro-typical, and consequently there was a desire to interview real-life Aspergers who had had social relationships and were willing and able to talk about them.

There weren't that many Aspergers available with experience of relationships and/or the readiness to discuss them. As I had at least managed to get it together with a girl once or twice, and had a former girlfriend who thought (and was willing to be quoted on the subject) that I was "more romantic and attentive than anyone she'd ever known, like something out of the movies,"

I was well able to produce some purple prose to order. I was also able to make clear that, like Adam, I didn't pick up social cues automatically and had to painstakingly learn the 'rules' of relationships. Paradoxically, in practice that meant I observed those rules more exactingly than a neuro-typical might.

In short order, I was interviewed by the *Sunday Herald*, *Scotland on Sunday*, the *Sunday Mail* and, most rewardingly, by Kate Hodal of the Press Association.

With every interview, my public speaking ability improved until, as a film critic once said of Sean Connery in *Never Say Never Again*, I was "purring lethally" and enjoying every moment of my fifteen minutes of fame.

For example:

James Christie was diagnosed with Asperger's syndrome seven years ago. A qualified librarian who lives in Glasgow, he has had a handful of romantic relationships with women, the longest lasting three months, but he struggles with the nuances of social intimacy. "There's an innate sort of alienation," he says. "You've got to get over the first barrier. The body language is innately different. I'm reluctant to make the first move and reluctant to trust my instincts. I'll be very conservative in trying to start a relationship."

Christie, who is 44, broke up with his last girlfriend 18 months ago. They remain in touch and Christie produces a clutch of notes to prove it. "I was more romantic and attentive than anyone she'd ever known," he says. "She said I should have women chapping on my door, that I was like something out of the movies, that I knew how to treat a lady."

... Christie is affable and articulate, but curiously inexpressive: his speech has only one register. On listening back to our conversation later on tape, I realise I've missed most of his jokes. He sprinkles his conversation with factual titbits and sometimes answers a question, out of the blue, from five minutes beforehand. Just as striking is Christie's ability to reel out strings of fully formed, unhesitant sentences.

(Gordon Darroch, *Sunday Herald magazine*, July 27 2009)

The National Autistic Society's latest Campaign, launching on Tuesday, is called Don't Write Me Off. Carol Evans, the society's director in Scotland, says: "Our report reveals that the majority of the more than 300,000 working-age adults with autism in the UK want to work but are being held back by a woeful lack of understanding among employment and benefits advisers at Jobcentre Plus and a dearth of specialist employment services."

... James Christie, aged 44, knows only too well how difficult it can be to earn a living. "I've had to wash toilets to stay in work," he says. "My earning potential is so low I get Christmas cards from the low pay unit."

... Aspergers also have a tendency to focus on a narrow range of interests. "I consistently wear the same style of clothes and eat the same type of food – pasta, tomatoes and Campbell's condensed soup every night for over two years."

... Christie gained an honours degree in humanities and a post-graduate degree in library and information studies; by his own admission he is highly intelligent, but climbing the ladder of success proved impossible. "I had several terrible career stumbles....Nobody could see why, on the one hand, I was so intelligent and why, on the other, I went to a certain level of job and ran straight into a brick wall."

It wasn't until 2002, when he was 37, that a breakthrough – or rather a breakdown – came. Taking his mother on holiday, the planning and logistics of it all became too much and, as he describes it: "I hit the wall. I couldn't go on. I was like a computer with screen freeze."

He then spent his entire holiday wondering: "Why did this happen to me?" Back in Britain, he read an article about the book An Asperger Marriage and saw some similarities with his own life. "I went to my GP and said, 'I don't think I could have this – I have a job and a flat in the city whereas my rough impression of autism is that essentially you can't hold down a job or live independently – but can you get me checked out anyway?"

(Ruth Walker, *Scotland on Sunday*, October 11 2009)

When James Christie offers you tea or coffee, it's not a good idea to say: "I'll have what you're having."

It may seem polite, or even "normal" small talk, but for James options can prove complicated and stressful.

The 44-year-old has Asperger's syndrome – a rare form of autism.

... That's why when I enter James' flat in Partick, Glasgow, and he asks whether I want coffee or tea, our conversation goes into meltdown.

My vague respons –"Only if you're making ... either is fine" sends him into a frenzy of confusion...

(Gayle Ritchie, Sunday Mail, October 26 2009)

When I was interviewed by Kate Hodal of the Press Association, we had a very good rapport and she seemed to understand my strange relationship with Drusilla:

"Most people have an autopilot, but having Asperger's means I don't," says 44-year-old James Christie.

Diagnosed with Asperger Syndrome, a rare form of autism, seven years ago, the Glasgow-based data assistant say he lives each day "by manual control".

It's not known exactly how many people suffer from the lifelong form of autism in the UK, but experts estimate as many as half-a-million.

Characterised by having difficulty with social interaction and communication, those with Asperger's find social cues which we all take for granted, such as body language and tone of voice, very difficult to understand.

"It's like the culture shock of being somewhere foreign all the time, except for the fact that I'm at home. I have to think, 'How do I say: Hello, how are you? How do I approach this, or any, situation?'," he explains.

It's a way of life that Christie, a charmingly eccentric and eloquent man with a penchant for science fiction, has got used to over the years.

But it has not been easy. Jobs and relationships have suffered because of his condition – with his inability to multi-task or read sexual cues infuriating managers and alienating potential girlfriends.

..."I don't like to talk about it very much. It was pretty awful. I didn't fit in, couldn't understand very much. I felt physically and emotionally alienated from the world."

Despite growing up in a family who worked in the health service – his mother is a former nurse and his father worked with adults with mental-health problems – Christie wasn't diagnosed until 2002, at the age of 37.

"I had no idea about autism except what I saw in Rain Man," he explains.

"My problems were too well hidden and the clues too well compensated for by my achievements in other areas to be noticed until many years later."

...It was only a chance reading of a newspaper article on Asperger's seven years ago, he says, that got him wondering whether there was a reason for his lack of social skills.

...A series of tests revealed that Christie is extremely articulate and has very good writing skills, but very poor information-processing abilities – a clear indication of Asperger's.

"That's why I like to say I'm part near-genius, part low-grade moron," he laughs, stressing that he still needs people to talk to him clearly and bluntly for him to properly understand.

The diagnosis has allowed Christie, who cares for his mother and is one of an estimated 13% of adults with an autism-spectrum disorder able to hold down a full-time job, to understand himself better.

Ritualising certain aspects of his life and not overworking his brain help him to live more comfortably with his condition.

"People with Asperger's do things in a certain way for reassurance because our ability to cope with the information flooding in from the outside world is severely limited," Christie explains.

"We need a routine and a narrow, limited range of interests to keep us focused: heavyweight boxing, Scottish history and Buffy the Vampire Slayer are mine."

...And – perhaps ironically for a guy with emotional detachment issues – Christie describes himself as "sentimental bag of mush at heart" who is still looking for "the one".

Sadly, and for no known reason, Asperger Syndrome is more common in males than in females. And having loved and lost just twice in his life, Christie is still struggling to find a girlfriend.

"I once was a natural loner and learned, without question, that the single life is not the way to be," he says.

"Courting and etiquette are a set of certain rules that can be learned over time, and I learned – painstakingly – how to be a good man in my last relationship.

"That said, I think it's a great pity that those who have the social skills I lack so often seem to squander them."

(Kate Hodal, Press Association, August 22 2009)

The greatest of journeys can have the smallest of starts. You may ask what impulse first set me on the road to Candlewood Drive, Point Lobos and the cypress trees on Sunset, and I could wax lyrical about quests, grails, road trips and my own personal Guineveres, but the truth was a little simpler than that.

My position in the organisation was still precarious. My new data entry post was temporary, but I had a permanent contract and the organisation still lacked a redundancy policy so they couldn't just fire me. I was awaiting redeployment, partly protected by the fact that the management were reluctant to tangle with a disabled person protected by UNISON, but I couldn't really plan ahead or think about the future with any confidence.

Then the chance of a cataloguing job at Glasgow's Mitchell Library came up and I thought:

If I get the job, why not take a holiday in the US and do a little personal PR for the NAS on the side?

And that's how it all began.

21

A trendy road-trip

From: Christie, James
Sent: 13 July 2009
To: Raemond Charles
Cc: James Doherty
Subject: RE: Pictures

Thanks for the pictures, Raemond.

Incidentally, had a not-exactly-serious-but-not-that-unlikely idea for a PR journey which might benefit NAS. I'll discuss it with Jim next time I see him, but it could work in concert with a trip I hope to make across America next year.

Regards,
J.

From: James Doherty
Sent: 14 July 2009 12.22
To: Christie, James
Subject: from broomhill to baton rouge

Hi James

Just back today after a great wee break. The old u.s. of a. eh? sounds great, are you planning some sort of road trip? Im already visualising you cruising past various American landmarks with the shades on and the wind in your hair...

Jim

Hi Jim

Glad you had a good break. I think it's liberated your inner poet. I also woke up to the fact that (on the whole) all PR is good PR. When I was researching locations for *Drusilla's Roses* I found a nature reserve near Monterey Bay called Point Lobos, which looked marvellous and Mediterranean and, as it had been 20 years since I was in California, I kind of got a hankering to go see it and do Steinbeck country, rather than just go to LA and pathetically try to get Juliet Landau's autograph.

So, it had been in my head awhile to:

1.   Fly to New York
2.   Hitch-hike across the continental United States to LA
3.   Attend a screening of Juliet Landau's independent short film *It's Raining Cats and Cats* and try and get her to sign a copy of *Roses*
4.   Go see the real Candlewood Drive
5.   Hitch-hike north via California Highway 1 to Point Lobos
6.   Return to UK from San Francisco

And if I'd got the Mitchell cataloguing job, that was the idea. Unfortunately, I got the rejection a couple of days ago but I'd still like to travel while I'm still young enough to do so.

While I was writing a human/vampire romance, however, I rather failed to noticed that this very genre has become the 'in thing' in Hollywood. Buffy's romance with Angel started it, it went global with Stephanie Meyer's *Twilight* series of novels/films and HBO is going to screen *True Blood* (a vamp/human romance set in Louisiana) on FX this Friday. Drusilla herself (written by Landau) is even returning shortly in a comic book series.

Funny, I write my story to give a neglected character a nice send-off and the whole genre resurrects itself around me...

So, it occurred to me that *if* I got some form of secure job, I could do the trip and, just as I did 20 years ago, write a sequence of articles en route giving an Asperger's view of America which could be serialised for the NAS and/or the media. Theoretically,

Miss Landau could be asked by the NAS to meet with me when I reached Los Angeles, and I think she might appreciate the publicity. Well, it all sounds a bit unreal in writing but I'm planning to do this anyway if I ever get the chance, and I have absolutely no objection whatsoever to raising the profile of Asperger's and the NAS if I can. There are also a lot of very intelligent *Buffy* fans out there, some of whom are probably in high places, and a trendy road trip like this might make some interesting connections and open some doors.

I'm not being *entirely* serious, but I'm certainly not joking either, and I've already got the experience of travelling and writing my way round the world.

Do you think this idea is viable and could be turned into good PR? Best wishes,
J.

From: James Doherty
Sent: 15 July 2009 10:00
To: Christie, James
Subject: RE: from broomhill to baton rouge

Hi James

On the face of it, it sounds like an extremely interesting PR exercise. As you say yourself, there are various 'angles' to this adventure which could be used to generate publicity. so from my own point of view it sounds a really great idea although being practical there would be a lot of factors/possibilities that would need to be taken into consideration.

Raemond would be best placed to advise you further on whether it would be something the NAS could be involved in – why not email him your ideas to see what he thinks?

We've moved from our old office back round into the main NAS corridor so I now have a half-decent view from the windows as opposed to looking onto a brick wall. I think that may also have stimulated my inner poet.

Jim

From: Christie, James
Sent: 15 July 2009 14:43
To: James Doherty
Cc: Raemond Charles
Subject: RE: from broomhill to baton rouge

Dear Jim

Glad you like the idea, and it's important to stress I was planning on doing it anyway, and that I've got the previous experience (Australia 1988-1989) to survive out there. When I first became suspicious that I had Asperger's, it did not seem possible that I could have coped with that trip, but I did.

I'd mainly worry about technical difficulties. Twenty years ago, I wrote articles on paper and mailed them home. Now I could take a laptop and write in real time, but a road trip *always* tests equipment to the limit and I have lurking fears that I might find myself in Hell west of Albuquerque, looking out upon Monument Valley from a mesa or something, all ready to put out peerless prose and find the ****** Wi-Fi link has gone down.

There is also the question of whether I would be physically up to life on the road again and it's also vitally important to remember America is a dangerous place with a rampant gun culture.

Nevertheless, to quote a Roman gladiator, "one does not survive the arena without some skills as deep as bone," and a year Down Under (returning via the US) certainly has prepared me for three weeks or so in modern-day America.

Well, for me, it all hinges on whether I can get a full-time salary from somewhere!

Last thoughts, my idea is a bit like "Rain Man," come to think of it. Although I'm more capable than Raymond Babbit and I'd be travelling alone, I would be going in the same direction...

Well, I'll copy this to Raemond and see what he thinks. I hope he's interested, and I can unearth my original articles from 20 years ago if he'd like to see what I did last time round.

Regards,
J.

From: Raemond Charles
Sent: 27 July 2009 10:25
To: Christie, James
Subject: RE: Adam Film Review

James

Glad you liked the piece – I thought it was really good and your interview excellent.

Yeah your idea sounds brilliant but as you said we need to have a look at it if and when you get the full time job, but we have time on our hands so that is a good thing for a change.

From: Christie, James
Sent: 27 July 2009 15:21
To: Raemond Charles
Subject: RE: Adam Film Review

Hi Raemond

Glad to know you think the idea has potential. Pity it all hangs on whether a full-time job is to be or not to be, but I wouldn't expect to be doing it before early next year anyway unless fate decides to show its hand. Mind you, I was cheerfully fantasizing about appearing on *David Letterman* assuming I got through to LA in one piece and I would seriously make the point that I'm perfectly able to appear before an audience. I seem to have inherited all of my father's natural speaking ability, as well as the knack of talking off the cuff. Pity about my one-note speaking style but I'll try and compensate for that.

Without being in any way facetious about Gary McKinnon's possible fate, it might also give the US a slightly better impression of Asperger's. I certainly would *not* be trying to compromise their national security!

Best wishes,
J.

At the time, I was sending emails from work because my knackered old dial-up internet account had given up the ghost. Unlike many Autists, I wasn't umbilically attached to the internet, so the loss of access was of no great concern to me; but it was one of those small details in which the devil lay, and it had the power to destroy everything.

22

Fifteen minutes of fame

I thought August 15 2009 was just another ordinary day and let it pass me by, unregarded. Despite my Asperger focus, I could not see every detail around me and there was one I missed.

At the time I was more interested in emailing Kate Hodal to try and get an unabridged copy of her article. I was enjoying my 15 minutes of fame, my small taste of celebrity. I could even Google myself.

From: Christie, James
Sent: Mon 8/24/2009 16:24
To: Kate Hodal
Subject: Aspergers, Press & Journal, 22nd August

Dear Mrs Hodal

Pleased to see article printed P&J 22nd, but I can't get a complete copy from their website. Any chance you could send me an unabridged copy?

Best wishes
James Christie
P.S. Thanks for mentioning Drusilla.

From: Kate Hodal
Sent: 25 August 2009 01:34
To: Christie, James
Subject: RE: Aspergers, Press & Journal, 22nd August

Hi James

My sincere apologies I haven't written sooner. I am currently on holiday in California!

I have found this copy:

http://www.theautimnews.com/2009/08/22/i-felt-out-of-place-in-this-world/

However, this is the full – not abridged – version, and it seems to be from the P&J.

Hope this helps a tad. Will email more as I see where else it goes.

Hope you and Drusilla are well!

Kate

From: Christie, James
Sent: Tue 8/25/2009 10:03
To: Kate Hodal
Subject: Aspergers, Press & Journal, 22nd August

Dear Kate

Thanks very much for the link. It now appears the *Sunday Mail* is after me, too, and I will try to sandwich Dru in amidst the serious stuff. It would be nice if someone associated with *Buffy* (ie Juliet Landau) noticed my relationship with everyone's friendly neighbourhood deranged vampire, but I'm hoping to do something about that early next year anyway. Still, she's in a good mood with me at the moment as I worked until 2.00 am this morning on the second Drusilla story. This is despite the fact I'm about to drop her into the Congo to (probable) certain death and round off the trilogy by batting her 20 years into the future with a swipe of a dragon's tail. Poor thing.

Trust you've had a good hol in California. I set part of *Roses* at Point Lobos State Reserve near Monterey and Steinbeck country, would love to see it in real life.

Best wishes,
James

From: Kate Hodal
To: Christie, James

Hi James

Wow! What great news.

There is actually a mention of Juliet Landau if you follow the autism news link all the way to the bottom (to the comments). Appears that a woman used to work with Landau and …

Well, you'll see soon enough.

Talk soon

Kate

You'll see soon enough…

Sometimes the smallest of words announce the greatest of changes.

I followed the link, and this is what I saw:

I work with Juliet Landau who played Drusilla on Buffy and we both read this story and were blown away by how good it was.

In that moment, the world changed.

Juliet Landau had read *Drusilla's Roses* and liked it, and now I knew it.

Up until then, Hollywood had been a dream. Now that dream was a little more real and the way to the sunlit city a wee bit clearer.

I began to feel better. I'd spent three years looking into the sad and empty workings of closed and ugly minds. A feeling akin to sitting in an empty pub at two in the morning soaked in the smell of stale beer and old cigarette smoke.

What relief then to open the door, walk out into clean desert dunes and look up to see, far away and shimmering in the haze, the sparkling spires of a city. Home to scholars, high culture and art.

And to hear the song on the wind, telling me to go out again.

23

Crossing a line

If Kirk could steal the *Enterprise*, Hornblower come alive on the deck of the deck of the *Hotspur*, and a Crusader walk through the desert to Jerusalem, what was I to do?

Well, I could send an email.

Miss Landau had a public business email address. Since I'd sent *Roses* to Hollywood, Meltha and I had revised its text slightly, changing some of my British idioms for Stateside jargon. Terms like 'breakfast bar' were swapped for 'kitchen island,' the distinctly American phrase 'wobbled like Weebles' (which referred to Hasbro's roly-poly toys from the 1970s, popularised by the slogan 'Weebles wobble, but they don't fall down') had been added, and together we'd created what I called the third (American) edition.

Why not send Miss Landau the third edition?

Why not, indeed?

I didn't think about it much at the time, but this was my first experience of dealing with a celebrity, and (as Hugh Grant had said to Julia Roberts in *Notting Hill*) it was indeed surreal. Sending the earlier edition of *Roses* with its covering letter had been an action passionately taken but professionally handled. I knew little of the person to whom I had written and did not expect to learn more. I had spent six months writing *Roses* with Dru at my flat in Partick, not with Juliet. Drusilla was a daffy, fictional vampire with whom I was intimately acquainted. Juliet was a sober, flesh and blood professional actress living in LA who scarcely knew I existed.

That was the way things had been, and the way I had disciplined myself to expect them to continue.

But now circumstances were changing. Juliet Landau knew I existed and I had a means of contacting her.

In my experience, the basic disconnect between the celebrity and the man in the street is this:

Time is out of sync.

When two ordinary people meet, they usually haven't seen each other before. Neither knows who the other is, they meet in the flesh and there is a simultaneous mutual appraisal.

In a celebrity's case, millions of men in the street have already seen images of her. Some of them may mistakenly think they know her, though they don't; and for her part she knows them not at all.

So the man may love the illusion, and the celebrity is blind.

I had first 'seen' Juliet in 2004, but she did not become aware of me until 2009. It had taken us five years even to begin to get in sync, and that was only due to a complex chain of luck, torment and circumstance.

Perhaps the first difference in dealing with a celebrity as opposed to the ordinary man in the street is that, however rationally and carefully you tell yourself that you are merely talking to a fellow human being who happens to work in the entertainment industry, there is nevertheless an inevitable feeling of awe. A flush of blood to the cheeks, a thrill of adrenalin to the system. A slightly giddy sense of disbelief as the real blends with the surreal and you begin to interact with and relate to someone who, up until that moment, had been an iconic image on the screen.

That is the first difference, the first psychological hurdle to overcome. Next, and no matter how carefully you try to avoid it, comes the fact that you will consider your actions more carefully as you get to know a celebrity. You defer a little more. You are more wary of causing offence. You know you are crossing a line into a world many others never see.

In a word, you aren't just going to walk up to a film star and say, "hi gorgeous, wanna get a cup of coffee?"

Perhaps being autistic is even an advantage in such a situation. Although my emotions were buffeting me, the logical Vulcan brain was firmly in command and guiding my actions rationally.

All the same, I was going into unexplored territory.

Two-fifteen in the afternoon. August 31 2009.

I sat at my desk in the real world and pondered what to do. Then I created a new email and began to write.

How to start?

Only one way.

Dear Miss Landau...

From: James Christie
Sent: 31 August 2009 14:15
To: Juliet Landau
Subject: Drusilla's Roses

Dear Miss Landau

Well, didn't think I'd be writing *that* again. Thought it more likely I'd end up down in the cells getting a kicking from the Glasgow Police, celebrity stalker squad. However, since I wrote *Roses* I seem to have become a very, very minor celebrity myself (in the area of autism, anyway) and was more than pleased recently to hear from Kate Hodal (who interviewed me for the Press Association) that her article had appeared in the *Autism News*. I think this is an American web site, and it seems that "deverill" blogged in reply to said article that she and yourself had read and rather liked *Roses*.

Shoot an arrow in the air, it may land I know not where...

24

A rare and delicate thing

The email went out. The world turned on its axis. Life went on its way. I went home from work. I don't remember what I did that night.

I went back to the office the next day, an anonymous person lost amidst a stream of others, passing unseen through the arteries of the city, private and obscure. I turned on the computer, checked my emails and found a reply in my inbox:

From: Juliet Landau
Sent: 31 August 2009 16:53
To: Christie, James
Subject: Re: Drusilla's Roses

Hi James

Thank you for letting me know what you are up to. Your ideas sound fantastic!

Best,
Juliet

Surreal, all right.

That wasn't a PA. That wasn't a standard response. That was *her*, tapping away from a keyboard 5,000 miles away.

Juliet Landau.

In Hollywood.

I stood up, went into the staff toilet, and swore. Then I went back to my desk, let the flush of adrenalin dissipate, rationally disciplined the sense of awe...

My God, that's her! That's really her!

Okay, *tried* to rationally discipline the sense of awe...

And composed a reply.

My God, I'm talking to her! I'm really talking to her!

Okay, calm down, bonehead. It's a correspondence. Just a correspondence.

Those wildfires they're having in LA sound dangerous, though.

Hope she's all right.

I sent a cautious response, asking after her health, hoping she wasn't being fried. Admitting I was happy to hear from her. She replied. I wrote again. She replied. Every Wednesday I went home from work and sweated it, wondering if I'd find a reassuring answer in my inbox on the Monday.

I always did.

I turned 45 on September 4 2009. Juliet even wished me a happy birthday. I took Mum down to Moffat for the day, and we found a toy museum in a little side-street.

There wasn't a collection of *Buffy* memorabilia amongst the exhibits, but there *was* a set of *Space: 1999* characters standing behind glass. Including Commander Koenig and Helena Russell, played by Juliet's parents Martin Landau and Barbara Bain.

I looked at the figures for a long while, thinking of a little girl who'd perhaps danced around the set of Moonbase Alpha's Main Mission long ago while I watched the show, unknowing.

Then, like a fool, I began to wonder if I was doing the right thing.

There was also the uncertainty and the pain.

If I seem to talk blithely of my experiences of relationships with words like 'taking punishment' and 'smashing my head through a plate-glass window,' do not, please, think I am treating the subject lightly or facetiously. I have even less idea about what's going on than the average man, and trying to work it out *hurts*.

The NAS definition of Asperger Syndrome states that we have difficulties in three main areas. They are:

- Social communication
- Social interaction
- Social imagination.

They are often referred to as the triad of impairments. In brief, and taking samples from the NAS definition, I was setting out on an online correspondence with difficulties expressing myself emotionally and socially, and in understanding the unwritten social rules that most people pick up without thinking. I also have a tendency to imagine alternative outcomes to situations and find it hard to predict what will happen next, and problems understanding or interpreting other people's thoughts, feelings or actions.

I'd given up relying on my social instincts years before, and to add even more complications to the trek upon which I seemed to be embarking, the correspondence was online, leaving me largely unable to work out analogy, subtext, tone, inflection or body language.

Nor was there much precedent for this kind of correspondence. Email and Twitter (I began to read Juliet's tweets a couple of months after we made contact) were very new forms of communication, and because of the constant danger of stalkers and obsessives which celebrities face it was probably pretty rare for one of them to be able to talk with and trust a member of the general public without being let down or even endangered.

I realised very quickly that I couldn't ask her address or much in the way of personal details, but also knew I was walking a fine line and that the correspondence was a rare and delicate thing.

Not only that, I'd spent six months with Drusilla in my head. Now I was dealing with her real-life counterpart who was a famous celebrity to boot. I wasn't even exactly sure who was who or which one was my favourite!

So I took advice: everyone said I should hold back, and like a lumpen idiot I listened to them.

Miss Landau's last reply lay unanswered in my inbox. I descended into a grump while everyone reassured me I'd done the right thing, so to alleviate my dark and dire mood I phoned home for a moan:

"Mum, I've dumped Miss Landau."

"Won't she be a bit put-out you've stopped talking to her?"

"Aw thanks, Mum. That's just what I wanted to hear..."

"I think she liked getting messages from you, dear, and now she'll be disappointed."

"Thanks, Mum..."

Autists sometimes have a reputation for acting immaturely, and I sure fitted the bill that time. I put the phone down, grouched off into the living room, tried to behave with dignity, tried not to mooch through a *Buffy* episode with you-know-who in it, tried not to stare moodily at the nearby wall, and failed on all counts.

But at least I'd done the right thing, or so everyone told me.

A month went by. My proposal to travel to the US remained with the NAS while its wheels turned slowly towards a decision and I stared moodily at the occasional wall. But I also began to remember what it had been like to travel.

Autists are often defined as 'Mr Spock' types. An excellent book on the subject by Barbara Jacobs is even entitled *Loving Mr Spock*, but there was a bit more Captain Kirk than Mr Spock in my nature. My own great-grandfather had even been a sea captain for the Burns Line, sailing out of Montrose. He skippered some transatlantic ships, and died in New York in 1899.

In the *Star Trek* episode *The Ultimate Computer*, Kirk once said, *"even if you take away the wind and the water, it's still the same. The ship is yours – in your blood you know she is yours – and the stars are still there to steer her by."* It remains true today.

There are some who must take to the sea or sky, or spend every moment of their lives regretting that they did not go.

"I'll try not to get hit by a Mack truck," I'd said several times to Jim, as the proposal was originally based on the idea of hitch-hiking across the continental United States.

I'd been joking, but I'd also been serious. Independent travel is very, very different from package holiday-making. There is no tour guide to keep you out of trouble. No luxury coach to shepherd you safely from place to place while you turn your brain off. No prearranged accommodation, and so on.

You are very heavily dependent on your own physical and psychological ability, and if you are not aware of what is going on around you, you have a very good chance of being conned, robbed, buggered or run over by something large and heavy, and coming home in a body bag.

In one terrible case many years ago, a young man from Aberdeen went on a business trip to Houston. Not quite realising he was no longer in Scotland, he went out with a mate and got plastered. He ended up drunk in a Houston suburb and banged on someone's door, the way he might have done at home.

Texas is not Scotland. In Scotland, the worst that would happen would be an altercation, a call to the police and maybe a night in the cells for breach of the peace. In Texas, home owners have (or had then) the legal right to defend their homes with lethal force. The young man went home in a body bag.

When I was passing through Los Angeles in 1989, I stayed a few nights at backpackers' hostel at Venice Beach. On arrival, I was quietly given one piece of advice:

Go on Venice Beach after 6.00 pm and you're dead.

I did not, not for one single second, either question that advice or ignore it because it did not fit my preconceptions. I stayed in, I stayed alive, and I came home in one piece.

The difference between living and dying abroad lies in how clearly you realise you are in a foreign country where the rules are different. As an Autist, I am perhaps better able to accept those rules than a neuro-typical, but it makes no difference which end of the spectrum you're on. Deal with the facts as they are, or they'll deal with you. I've lost count of the number of tourists I've met who wander around vaguely saying things like, "it's not like this in Scotland/England/Europe/America," thinking with their emotions and not really dealing with the fact they're not on their home turf any more.

This inability to get the message extends to the highest levels of government. In his memoir of life as Britain's ambassador to the US, *DC Confidential*, Christopher Meyer explicitly stated:

> *'Every year, in September, I used to address new arrivals at the embassy, with their families. The core of my message was always the same: think of the US as a foreign country; then you will be pleasantly surprised by the many things you find in common with this most generous and hospitable of peoples. Think of America as Britain writ large and you risk coming to grief; American attitudes to patriotism, religion, crime and punishment, schooling, sex, the outside world, can be very different from those of Europeans, including the British. For the novice British diplomat it comes as a shock to discover that most Americans, whether Republican or Democrat, sophisticate or redneck, believe that their country's actions in the world are intrinsically virtuous; and more fool those countries that do not recognize this. The attitude of Britain's Victorians was very similar.*
>
> *I sought regularly and in vain to get the Foreign Office to grasp this message and to draw the conclusion that if it was right to train cadres of specialists in the EU, the Middle East, Russia and China, as we do, then it was also right to create an American cadre, which we do not do.'*

Nowadays, even I have noticed a rash of rapes and murders of young people abroad who, instead of keeping their eyes and ears open, jabbered manically away on their mobiles and consequently got done over by the locals.

Independent travel is a young person's game, though, and I'd had my day in the 1980s. Furthermore, I now knew that my psychological ability – the inner core which had enabled me to cope with the accelerated stress and changes that travel entails – was compromised.

I knew I was middle-aged. I knew I was autistic, and I knew that I just might not have it any more. This can happen to elite athletes. One day they're at the top of their form. The next, they've lost it. They will still pass any physical or neurological test but the edge is gone, and cannot be regained.

I knew perfectly well that those 'skills deep as bone' of which I'd talked to Jim might have withered on the vine, but I still wanted to go out there.

And if there is a fate and destiny waiting for us all, sometimes there are signs.

Round about then, I was driving down a long straight stretch of road past Tinto Hill in the Upper Clyde Valley when I saw, real as real could be, a Mack truck.

Not a vision and not a dream, the real thing.

Perhaps it had been displayed at Biggar's Albion Foundation Rally. Perhaps a local enthusiast had restored it and let it loose to enjoy the sunshine on a good day. Perhaps it was all coincidence, but I was there that day and I saw it.

Of course, one shouldn't take signs too seriously. They are open to a variety of interpretations.

It might mean I would hitch-hike across the US.

It might also mean I would get hit by a Mack truck.

Something to look forward to...

In the meantime, while I waited for decisions to be made and events to begin to move, I decided I might as well get broadband.

It wasn't as if Juliet Landau would email me, though.

Of course not.

25

Sometimes there are signs

After losing my order three times, billing me wrongly and leaving me hanging on the telephone longer than Blondie, BT finally delivered broadband unto me. For them, that was quite efficient. For me, it was the kind of options-riddled neuro-typical nonsense which makes many Autists want to go hide in a corner.

It is difficult enough for us to make sense of the world when things are clear, consistent and transparent; damnable when the world is unclear, inconsistent and opaque.

It is no fun for neuro-typicals either, but for Autists it is even worse.

Finally, though, I was hooked up to the wired world, and as the BT engineer was leaving, he mentioned he'd been able to give me access to my old dial-up email account.

I am glad he did. Events might have turned out a little differently otherwise.

Late on a stygian Friday evening early in October, I took a look at my obsolete account.

I scrolled down through the 75 or so emails stagnating in the inbox, deleting some, not really concentrating on the job but still doing it with autistic precision.

Then I saw something.

An email from Juliet Landau, dated August 15 2009.

The 15th?

The 15th!

Two weeks before I'd emailed *her*!

With the care of a librarian handling the Book of Kells, I opened the email:

From: Juliet Landau
Sent: 15 August 2009 03:57
To: James Christie
Subject: Your Story

Dear James

I just finished your story. I thought it was great. I really enjoyed it. You managed to catch Drusilla's voice and behavior so beautifully. The sad, lost, haunted feeling of Dru was there. I myself have just written a comic about Dru as part of season 6 of "Angel." Please check it out if you'd like.

I sat there for a full five minutes, deciding what to do.

Take the advice and hold back, or take a shot in the dark and reply?

Sometimes there are signs.

I felt a quite a lot like Marty McFly at the *Enchantment Under The Sea* dance in the time-travel film *Back to the Future Part II*. He and I, both at a turning point between two alternate futures and not sure which road to take.

Reply. Something *might* happen.

Hold back. Nothing will happen.

In the end, I came to a simple decision.

Juliet Landau had been kind enough to email me. It would be impolite not to at least reply.

So, with the click of a mouse, I summoned the future:

From: James Christie
Sent: 03 October 2009 00:16
To: Juliet Landau
Subject: Re: Your Story

Dear Miss Landau

I'm sorry to be so tardy in replying, but I have only just retrieved your original email from my old cache and thought I really should respond.

Must mention I've now been interviewed by the *Sunday Mail* and *Scotland on Sunday*, and interviews should be coming out October/ November. In both cases I've talked about dear old Dru but will only mention these emails if OK'd.

I am glad you came through the fires all right. I hope to hear from you, and can provide further comments on Angel 24/25 if you wish.

With my best wishes,

James Christie

From: Juliet Landau
Sent: 03 October 2009 02:25
To: James Christie
Subject: Re: Your Story

Hi James,

I am in Hawaii on vacation.

It is beautiful here!

You can definitely mention our correspondence…

I'm off to the beach!!

All my best,

Juliet

And just like that, she was back.

26

The beast wants westering

A part from being autistic, which gave me enough problems, I'd come to maturity towards the end of the era of militant feminism, when it seemed a girl would kick you in the slats if you opened the door for her. I'd lived through the Bridget Jones era (where it seemed women wanted the life of a singleton, the high voltage career and the chance to see the world, but they also wanted to get married first). And I'd seen the other side of equality, meeting a nice girl, hoping for a caring relationship, then suddenly being told she was *afraid of commitment.*

You couldn't make it up. I had sat there in slack-jawed bewilderment listening to the classic excuse of the male commitment-phobe coming from the lips of a *female*. That was the last straw, so while the cataclysmic changes in relationships between the genders went on, I went past 40 and got tired of the whole thing.

Now, though, I'd been gifted with a second chance to talk to a nice pleasant lady who did not want to kick me in the slats, fly to Bangladesh or (I suppose) fear commitment. So what if she just happened to be a Hollywood star?

Drusilla had been kind, quiet and supportive. An old-fashioned feminine girl, if you excused the homicidal tendencies. The kind of lady you'd like to take out to dinner, even though you knew she'd feel obliged to try and make you the dessert.

Juliet seemed much the same as Drusilla, albeit bouncier, livelier and presumably less homicidal. I found I liked her, although I lived in fear that one day she would not reply.

I also sat fretting, waiting for the call to arms from the NAS, or not as the case might be.

The promise of a smile

x

97

I'd read John Steinbeck's books years before, and as I waited I remembered a tale of his in a book called *The Red Pony*. About an old man who'd been the leader of the people. A man who'd led the settlers across the Great Plains to the shores of the Pacific. It was as if he'd been born to do that one thing, but it came too early, and when he did it his life was done. So, forever after the crossing, he bored his family rigid by telling them the same tales of thieving Piutes and the failure to carry iron plates which cost lives during Indian attacks.

Then one day, he'd changed the record and told his grandson what it had really been like. Not the tired old tales of Piutes and plates, but how it felt to be young and alive to the roots of his soul. Burying the dead, burning in the sun, and in the end walking down to the sea with the tears fresh on his face:

' "It wasn't Indians that were important, nor adventures, nor even getting out here. It was a whole bunch of people made into one big crawling beast. And I was the head. It was westering and westering. Every man wanted something for himself, but the big beast that was all of them wanted only westering. I was the leader, but if I hadn't been there, someone else would have been the head. The thing had to have a head. Under the little bushes the shadows were black at white noonday. When we saw the mountains at last, we cried – all of us. But it wasn't getting here that mattered, it was movement and westering. We carried life out here and set it down the way those ants carry eggs. And I was the leader. The westering was as big as God, and the slow steps that made the movement piled up and piled up until the continent was crossed. Then we came down to the sea, and it was done." He stopped and wiped his eyes until the rims were red. "That's what I should be telling instead of stories." '

I'd gone out to Australia before. That beast inside me had made me go, and I'd known that if I didn't, I'd have been a nervous wreck by the age of thirty. That first trip should have killed me. It nearly had, but I'd made it back and forced myself into that quiet life of desperation because I felt I should.

But the beast still wanted westering and was dragging me to my feet once more. It did not care whether I was old or tired or weak. Even if I walked or crawled, it would force me on again, stumbling towards that glint of gold on the horizon. The azure shimmer promising sea, if only I could cross the dry-as-parchment land.

I did not hear the words clearly then, but they had made men march under banners and eagles and flags. For hope or glory or just the promise of a smile. An old and angry creed forgotten and foresworn, once ease and progress smoothed the way. Words which had no meaning to those who sat and watched but never moved:

Get up.

Get on your feet.

One last time.

From: Christie, James
Sent: 06 October 2009 13:22
To: James Doherty
Subject: Go for US?

Dear Jim

… I would *love* to be able to formally notify her that I will be doing this trek across the US so I would like to make a formal decision concerning that ASAP. I stress that I am not losing my head but I have to get in shape, get my passport renewed, negotiate unpaid leave with my line manager, and possibly get a Saturday shift at the Complex so I can start saving…

Best wishes
J.

From: James Doherty
Sent: 06 October 2009 14:00
To: Christie, James
Subject: RE: Go for US?

Hi James

Could you manage 1.30? We could perhaps head round to Morton's (coffee/hot choc on me).

Jim

October 14 2009. 1.30 pm.

The best moments in life are melodramatic. Like two wise old viziers smoking opium from hookahs, Jim and I shared coffee and chocolate at Morton's, a blue and white café halfway down Byres Road.

Technically, there were supposed to be other subjects for discussion, but all I really wanted to know was if I could travel again. There was only one flight to America from Glasgow airport, and if I didn't book at least three months ahead, I wasn't going.

"Do I have a 'go'?" I asked, consciously adopting the military parlance of my ancestors. 'Go' to commit to the operation. 'Abort' to stand down.

"As long as you don't try to hitch. We don't want you to get hit by a Mack truck."

"No problem. I'll take a Greyhound bus. See the real America. Do I have a 'go'?"

"Yes," Jim said. "You have a 'go.'"

27

The 72-hour rule

I'd love to say I came away from the meeting at Morton's walking on air, and that is partly true. But there was also the grim reality of preparation facing me, and once I'd got myself ready, I knew what setting off into the wide blue yonder and landing somewhere new would feel like.

As a callow 24-year-old, I'd arrived in Perth, Western Australia, in October 1988, and in short order realised:

1. Exactly how far away I was from home.
2. Exactly how long it would be before I got back.
3. Exactly how tenuous my situation was (no job, shelter or precise plan).

Not knowing I was autistic and ashamed of my fear of leaving home, I had decided on some drastic shock therapy. Most of us love and need routines, and I've seen fellow Autists petrified by the sight of an unfamiliar set of stairs. For an undiagnosed Autist, turning up at Perth International Airport was the equivalent of sailing off the edge of the planet (hell, Perth virtually *was* on the edge of the planet), and just as scary.

How did I cope with the shock of the change?

If you're looking for an easy answer, look elsewhere.

Call it the 72-hour rule. It will take the average person three days to adjust to the change, and during those three days you will be scared witless, near to crying like a child, and/or quite close to throwing up from sheer fear. You've just found out how big the universe really is and how small you are compared to it, and there's nothing else to do except suffer through it. Quite a few people quit in those 72 hours. I heard of one Mancunian family who were actually supposed to be emigrating to Perth. They turned tail and ran back home after two days, and I can't say I have much sympathy for them. Those three days are a test of character, and it brutally weeds the wheat from the chaff.

For me, the test felt like the kind of beating Rocky Balboa took from Apollo Creed in the first two rounds of their rematch. Creed wanted to demolish Balboa quickly to prove the first fight (where Balboa took him the distance) had been a fluke. Balboa's trainer, Mickey, warned him: "Now, he's gonna try to kill you quick. You get through this first round and he's *ours!*"

Balboa duly got beaten half to death for the first couple of rounds, but started coming on strong by the end of the second.

Although I was not being physically punched all over the ring, getting through the first 72 hours after landfall was its psychological equivalent. There was no easy way round it. I just hung in there until the fear subsided and the logical routines of my brain took command again. I then began to learn the rules of the road the hard way.

I wasn't going out for a year this time, of course, and I wouldn't have to go back to being a slave on a banana plantation, but experience can be a double-edged sword. I was *scared*, because I knew it was going to hurt.

Well, only one thing to do. Make the preparations, get back in shape, and hope for the best. To get myself in shape, I'd have to go back to the gym.

The boxing gym, funnily enough.

But at least now I had Miss Landau to talk to. The thought was comforting:

From: James Christie
Sent: 15 October 2009 14:10
To: Juliet Landau
Subject: Re: Your Story

Dear Miss Landau

Thank you very much for the emoticon (didn't quite know what it was at first and thought you'd sent me a colon); must admit I've had a look at your tweets now I've got broadband and am sorry to hear you came back to LA culture shocked and jet-lagged to a million emails and a malfunctioning computer.

Well, for the record, we did all miss you and we're glad you're back.

I tried to get you some column inches in the *Scotland on Sunday* article but no luck. Yet. I have attached the article for your interest, though.

Best wishes,

James

From: Juliet Landau
Sent: 15 October 2009 19:37
To: James Christie
Subject: Re: Your Story

Thanks James

Congrats on the article! I look forward to reading it! :)

(smiley face not a colon!!!!!)

Juliet

28

Back to the heavy bags

Every storm has its eye, and the Kelvin is Govanhill's. In a neighbourhood once christened 'Scotland's murder capital,' which is home to so many cultures that the local nursery school has children from 22 countries and where blonde Glaswegian tenements contrast with Asian shopfronts, the Kelvin Amateur Boxing Club stands for equality. A lawyer from Hyndland might rub shoulders with an ex-alcoholic from Pollok or a migrant from Kurdistan between the heavy bags hanging from the rafters of the former police station.

The Kelvin's twin mantras are discipline and respect, and any aspiring 'hard man' who struts through the door soon has his tough-guy attitude jabbed away.

I'd seen the worst side of humanity at the organisation but I'd met the finest of men at the Kelvin, and though the club itself iced-up in winter and boiled in summer, it was always a good place to be. The only thing no one could ever explain was why a boxing club on the Southside had a picture of a skier on the wall with the number 69 on his chest...

I'd trained there between 1998-2004, before my ill-fated sojourn at Nurse Ratched's cataloguing agency. Not fighting, not sparring, just punching. On my father's side, punching had always been part of family life. My father was born into the Army in India and first fought in public at the age of seven. My grandfather was the perfect soldier, surviving two world wars and raiding into Norway in his fifties in the second. In his hands, a Lee-Enfield rifle became an instrument of execution. He was one of the best shots in the world, and if he had you in his sights you were already a dead man.

Once, just once, my father said to me that we were a warrior caste, and I knew it. Fighters, soldiers, even noble knights – all were just variations on the theme of martial valour. I had no comprehension of football or rugby. I couldn't tell you what the offside rule was if my life depended on it, nor – despite thirteen years experience of life in Glasgow – did I even know in which stadia Rangers and Celtic played.

But I knew boxing, partly because my father had, out of habit, taught me how to fight. I found a natural interest in its rules and history, studying Muhammad Ali and the heavyweights, loving the idea of a big man moving light and fast on his toes, and as I filled out and reached six feet four, my feet had stayed light and I'd developed a punch in either hand.

Most people with Asperger Syndrome also tend to suffer from dyspraxia, or physical clumsiness. In my opinion, as the autistic brain has to do so much work just to haul its body through the day, it doesn't have the spare time to deal with the finer points of co-ordination unless a conscious effort is made, backed up by thousands of hours of practice.

This is why it really is a waste of time trying to involve people with Asperger Syndrome in team sports. I would say that the fine motor control is just not there so, for an Asperger, playing in a team is nothing more than a useless exercise in slow humiliation. To this day, I tend to say that I do not have *reflexes* but *reactions*. While the hardwired autonomic reflexes (breathing, opening and closing the eyelids etc.) are the same as a neuro-typical's, I believe that when my brain tries to tell my body how to balance, move and co-ordinate the movements of my limbs, it has to make a much more conscious effort to do so than an NT brain would.

Put another way, if I hit you with a jab, you know I've really thought about it.

However, if you practice long and hard enough, I believe the repetition can help the autistic brain iron out some of the dyspraxia, but it's a hard road. As a rule of thumb, people with autism would have to practice ten times as much as NTs to grind poise and balance into the central nervous system. I did put the hours in and now consider my clumsiness to be virtually invisible, but I have my limitations. Unlike neuro-typicals, I cannot do fancy tricks with a skipping rope. I can jump rope in time, but that's all.

I hadn't trained at the club for five years and I was seriously out of practice. But if there was one place which could (in *Rocky's* words) take me back like I was before, it was the Kelvin. Charlie Kerr, a former Scottish bantamweight champion, had been the backbone of the Kelvin ABC. He'd sparred with the great Jackie Paterson and seen Benny Lynch the day he died. I got to know Charlie when I first went to the gym. I'd trained for a while, then disappeared for seven months. When I returned, Charlie asked where I'd been. I told him my father had died. He sat with me for a while, talking with me. I never forgot that. There's a mural of him on the wall now, behind the heavy bags. He died in 2004, not long after I left.

Now I was back. I hadn't taken any exercise in two years and God knows what damage the accumulated stress of the last five years had done to me.

Could I get in shape again?

Only one way to find out.

I wrapped my hands, limbered up gingerly and headed over to the heavy bags. I didn't feel too bad, but that didn't mean anything. Hitting the heavy bag was the hardest exercise. Any weakness in the body would be exposed as 600 pounds of force in either hand hit the target and the recoil rippled through the skeleton. Hit the bag incorrectly and you risk a broken wrist or finger.

I tapped the bag a couple of times, trying to get the old reactions going, then threw a real punch.

And it was as if I'd never been away.

Fighting my way back to fitness under Charlie Kerr's watchful eye

From: James Christie
Sent: 18 November 2009 16:01
To: Juliet Landau
Cc: James Doherty
Subject: Re: Drusilla's Roses

Dear Miss Landau

I have some good, or at least interesting news. As you may recall, I submitted a PR idea to the NAS involving Drusilla and a trek across America (to be undertaken by me) with the aim of publicising Asperger Syndrome. Well, I was asked not to say anything until the idea was approved, but now it has been, so I expect to be in California about next March, barring any accidents.

Er, I do hope this isn't too much of a surprise. I know you've got a lot on at the moment.

Best wishes

James

From: Juliet Landau
Sent: 18 November 2009 16:18
To: James Christie
Subject: Re: Drusilla's Roses

Congratulations James!

That is very exciting!

Keep me posted!

Best,

Juliet

I thought a lot about the trip as I trained, but less about Candlewood Drive.

29

Enter Juliet the Notebook

It is very easy for those who have always had jobs and money to lecture others less fortunate:

"Just get a job!"

What do you think I'm going to do? Pick one up at the supermarket? I can't just go out, grab someone assertively by his lapels and shake it out of him! I have to apply, pray to reach the shortlist, drill myself through the usual daft answers to nonsensical interview questions, then nine out of ten times get rejected.

"Why don't you just *do* something?"

Without money, food, backing or shelter? Initiative alone won't do it, you pompous windbag...

"Do you really *want* to work?"

Well, let's see. I've spent 25 years living either in fear of, or on, the dole. I've been made redundant, humiliated, had my hopes dashed, nearly tortured into a nervous breakdown, seen achievements I cherished dumped and on the whole, only gained satisfaction from projects I either did privately or for free. Do I really look forward to unrewarding work or the deeply soul-destroying search for same? No I don't.

Such conversations usually end with my knee in the windbag's genitals as he tries to lecture me some more. I do not like people who blithely assume things will come together with the effortlessness of gods, but nor did I refuse to dream. Now I'd been given the go-ahead, and although there were still obstacles, something always came along to solve them. Not for one single moment, though, was the process ever effortless.

The NAS couldn't lend me a laptop upon which to write the articles?

Fine! I'll do it the old-fashioned way and use pen, paper and postage!

Out of the blue my cousin Keith Erskine, resident in Chicago, weighed in with the gift of a Notebook plus Wi-Fi subscription, as well as a temporary US cell phone.

Scarcely enough money to afford the trip?

Fine! I'll sleep in dormitories and overnight on Greyhound buses like I did last time!

My mother stepped in with financial aid. Perversely, one of her funds had done quite well out of the credit crunch and increased in value by £3,000.

There were other complications. The world had become a much more paranoid and bureaucratic place since 9/11, when a whole generation was brutally reminded that war was not on the way out and aircraft could become terrorist weapons. Travellers from the UK with full passports attempting to go to America under the Visa Waiver Program now also needed to get through the US Department of Homeland Security's electronic system of travel authorisation (ESTA). If they were not authorised by ESTA at least 72 hours before departure, not only would they not be allowed to enter the US, they would not even be allowed onto the plane *in the UK*.

I had the passport, but under the terms of the Program I could only travel as a tourist in the States. As the original aim of the journey included interviews and PR, a little warning bell started jangling in my head.

I phoned the US embassy in London, and in short order learned that to do any such thing I would have to be interviewed for a visa in Belfast or London (the US consulate in Edinburgh no longer offered this service). If I passed the interview, the visa could take up to 90 days to process. There was also the possibility that I might *not* pass the interview, in which case no visa and no trip to America.

As I would have to book at least 90 days ahead to secure a seat on the only daily flight from Glasgow to the US, this just wasn't going to work.

Having a reasoned, mature and sensible discussion about the US trip with Raemond Charles, the NAS Scotland PR guy

Not only that, US customs had the absolute authority to refuse entry. So, although it wasn't a life-or-death situation, I had to pass ESTA, falsely enter the US as a tourist and cope with customs.

I'd quipped I was a blunt instrument with a licence to kill from the NAS. Now I would technically have to enter the US undercover. Once on foreign ground, potential interviewers could contact me via my cell phone and if they did, well, it would be most impolite for me not to reply...

Cloak and dagger? Not really. More a way of coping with badly designed bureaucracy, and although it was quite fun to play James Bond, it should also have been quite unnecessary.

Although this nonsense might have fazed some Autists, I was quite sanguine about it. I had navigated US customs 21 years before: it had been the most polite grilling I'd ever had, and with my then-unknown Asperger focus fully in command, I'd sailed through.

This time, knowing that a characteristic of autism is the masked and unreadable face, I would use that very face to avoid giving anything away.

It was also decided not to inform Miss Landau of the undercover aspects of the operation until I was, as I put it, "wheels up and in the air." I reluctantly agreed with the decision. I trusted her, but the post 9/11 world seemed to be profoundly paranoid, and if one chance remark reached US Homeland Security, my trip might be over before it began.

It's worth repeating that, in some ways, the autistic mindset is better-suited to travel because it enables a person more clearly to comprehend the facts as they are and not (like some neuro-typicals do) as they wish them to be.

So I clearly got the message that:

- No ESTA, no departure.
- Fail at customs, no arrival.

I sometimes think that many neuro-typicals believe that there is an endless range of options, that something can always be 'worked out,' and that airport security rules can be broken at a whim. I pity the poor staff who have to tell them otherwise.

Now I was navigating the framework through which I had to slip. As well as my licence to kill, my passport had been renewed, my ESTA authorisation granted, my Notebook (called Juliet when it demanded a name during registration) had arrived, my seat on Continental Airlines flight CO17 had been booked for the first of March, returning (fittingly enough) on April Fool's Day, and a 30-day Greyhound Discovery Pass (a ticket to ride anywhere in America by bus) purchased.

Bearing in mind the importance of keeping US customs happy by having an address to go to upon arrival, I booked in at the Gershwin (a boutique hotel on East 27th Street in Manhattan) which, with an eye on the young independent travelers market, offered six- or eight-bed dorms as a cheaper alternative to single or double rooms. I had not slept in hostels, bunkhouses or dormitories for years and had no nostalgia for the sound of farts in the night or the pleasure of finding my bed had been reallocated and having to sleep on the floor. However, I knew I would be partly living off my mother's money for the month of March so I wasn't going to squander it.

Fools do indeed rush in where wise men fear to tread, I thought. *What a fool I am, and how very good it feels.*

From: James Christie
Sent: 22 December 2009 14:32
To: Juliet Landau
Subject: Re: The Collapse of Britain

Dear Miss Landau

Thought I better email sooner rather than later, or more precisely before the whole country comes to a grinding halt.

Just to say that, although the snow may be beautiful, the frost effervescent and the blue of the sky clear enough to make the very skin tingle, I think you'd probably find it a little chilly, to say the least.

I hope your ankle's better. The NAS PR man broke his in three places about the same time you hurt yours: these things always happen in threes and my right ankle started complaining in the gym last night, but it ended up behaving itself and I seem to be vaulting back to my former fitness.

But just in case Britain really does collapse over Christmas (I *think* I'm only joking), I just wanted to break slightly with my usual etiquette and say the most important thing, which is:

Merry Christmas, Juliet!

Best wishes

James

From: Juliet Landau
Sent: 23 December 2009 02:44
To: James Christie
Subject: Re: The Collapse of Britain

Thank you James.

Happy holidays to you!

:)

Juliet

30

Beware the Ides of March

How to keep your feet upon the ground when your head is 'midst the stars? How to keep your composure when you're kicking your way clear of the mire of Scottish winter, alive with frantic hope that you will indeed slip those surly bonds that tie us to the earth, take flight to the new world with its new frontiers and see once more palm trees on half-forgotten foreign shores?

Certainly not with the effortlessness of a god. However carefully I navigated my way past the traps, the bureaucracy seemed like a particularly surly tie to earth, intent only on irritation and obstruction.

To the bank:

"So even if I notify you in advance that I'm going abroad, you'll probably cancel my debit card anyway if I try to use it over there?"

"There's just so much fraud around, sir, that..."

"...That you've got a bunch of trigger happy 20-year-olds in your fraud department who'll shoot first and ask questions later?"

"Yes, sir!"

To the NAS IT guy:

"So, let me get all this jargon – which I can hardly even spell, let alone pronounce – right. I need an external CD drive to get the digital camera software onto the Notebook?"

"Yes."

"Do you have an external CD drive?"

"No."

To Jim, on finding out with three weeks to go before my March departure date, that Miss Landau was slated to attend the Cyprus Film Festival between March 25 and 28:

"March! March! *I'll be over* there *in March!"*

"Yes."

"Why the hell did I decide on March! Hell, buggery and beware the Ides of March! You mean that while I'm going there, *she'll be coming* here, *and by the time I reach California, she'll probably be in Cyprus?"*

"Yes."

"Aw, fu-..."

To a fellow traveller (actually on the airport bus on the way into Manhattan):

"What do you mean, the American banks don't like travellers' cheques any more! What am I supposed to do? Buy a bunch of greenbacks in the UK and shove them up my back passage?"

"Probably."

It was insane. I had found I could not rely on my cards so I'd gone back to the traditional old standby of travellers' cheques, only to find the US banks were getting sniffy about changing them. I felt like I, the Autist, was sane and the neuro-typical world crazy. It did in fact seem nutty but true that neuro-typicals, not Autists, had created a relatively inflexible facts-based world which then drove most of them mad with frustration much of the time.

My neuro-typical friends, however, were very supportive. They made several kind and insightful comments about the trip, my mental state, and the possible outcomes:

"James, does Martin Landau know you're stalking his daughter?"

"Who do you think you are, Forrest Gump?"

"Are you out of your Vulcan mind?"

"I'm not sure if you're crazy for going or she's crazy for agreeing to meet you!"

As the quiet frenzy of preparation continued, though, we began to realise that I might be a few weeks away from becoming the first Asperger in history to make and record a trip overland across the United States. The journalist Alistair Cooke took a similar trek in the 1940s. His manuscript, *Alistair*

Cooke's American Journey, was then lost and rediscovered in 2005. In the foreword, the editor, Harold Evans (writing in 2005) stated that:

> *"Only a handful of Americans have seen the country like that, still less reflected on its diversities. There is nothing weird about the doctor he meets in St Louis who tells him 'I never was west of Louisville nor east of Charleston, West Virginia.' "*

So relatively few people had done such a trip. Even fewer had kept a log, and as far as the NAS knew, no Asperger had ever done so. The record, written *en route,* would be sent back to the NAS in Glasgow and transferred to the NAS Events Facebook page, a bit like copy being filed from the frontline.

Crucial meetings in the NAS briefing room came and went as the clock ticked down to zero hour. There was a strange contrast between being personally fond of someone with whom I was corresponding in private and professionally dispassionate about her in public as a celebrity and focus for the trip.

Asperger Syndrome is sometimes nicknamed 'Engineer's Syndrome,' essentially meaning that male Aspergers like myself have exaggerated masculine characteristics. I'd love to say that means we are all strong silent types who look like John Wayne or Clint Eastwood and radiate intense sexual magnetism but that, unfortunately, is not the case. In essence, we have a greater tendency to be interested in fixing technical or mechanical problems, less ability to empathise emotionally and are more able to compartmentalise aspects of our lives. A form of shutting down or going into our 'caves' which I believe women dislike intensely.

Oddly enough, although I was able to compartmentalise my personal feelings and professional detachment about Juliet Landau, and although it probably made me better able to cope with the unique strain of knowing a celebrity, I didn't particularly enjoy the process.

She was a human being, not a project or a target, and I liked her. I was having to learn how to do so, of course, pressing long-unused emotional parts of my personality back into service, running the data I was receiving through the facts-based grinders of my mind and trying, with what little maturity and experience I had, to handle our correspondence.

How very paradoxical it all was. The less able autistic man acknowledging and trying to understand social relationships more readily than the supposedly more gifted neuro-typical.

Perhaps the moral of the story is that those who have things handed to them on a plate often squander the riches so easily received whereas those less fortunate, who have had to beg for scraps and leavings, savour every sip of the wine that nourishes their soul.

Even more paradoxically, a hack journalist might write a story based on the events I was now living, placing the hero midway between two women: the Hollywood star and the ordinary girl next door. The star would be depicted as a fame-obsessed shrew and the girl next door as the disregarded jewel, sweet and shy. At the end, the lunk-headed hero would realise the star was shallow and empty beneath the façade of her glamour, finally notice the girl next door's sterling qualities and marry her, leaving the star to pursue worthless roles in a bitter life of soulless rejection.

Life, however, was not really like that.

I should know. I'd known the girl next door, and what a selfish little shrew she'd turned out to be.

The Hollywood star, on the other hand, was coming across as kind, sweet, sensible and shy.

You really couldn't make it up.

For a' that, though, Jim and I had to be relentlessly dispassionate and consider all options. I'll never forget one bleak exchange in an otherwise empty boardroom.

"What if you get there," Jim said, "and she freaks out – refuses to meet you?"

I thought about it for a moment, knowing that every traveler had to hope for the best but plan for the worst. In 1969

Michael Collins, piloting Apollo 11's command module in lunar orbit, had been given alternate strategies to follow in case Neil Armstrong and Buzz Aldrin were unable to return from the surface.

I wasn't going that far, but to reach the Pacific coast and not see her...

"I'd put her birthday present in the post office. Then I'd go on and look at Candlewood Drive and Point Lobos," I said.

That was the end of *that* meeting.

Testing the camera in the Renfield Street Starbucks
where Drusilla's Roses *began*

31

Stealing the *Enterprise*

If a ship is the repository of our hopes and dreams, then the moment it sets sail is the greatest of days. The hope held close against the chest like fragile amethyst expands like a starburst in a faraway nebula, and the voyage has begun.

Hornblower had the *Hotspur* and Kirk the *Enterprise*. Both were commanders and their ships were of the line but, as a captain might say, sometimes the bonds between shipmates transcend the disciplines of the service. Kirk stole the *Enterprise* to save Spock. I would have done the same, but I was crossing the world for a different reason.

The early hours of March 1 2010. The obsessive rituals of preparation finally at an end. The taxi booked to take me to Glasgow airport at six-thirty in the morning. My rucksack standing ready by the rocking chair in the living room. My walking boots and all-weather coat waiting in the hall. I would put my passport in its holder around my neck in the morning.

The flat was quiet as a chapel, the fate I'd fought for finally upon me, and if Drusilla was there she was keeping her own counsel. Perhaps someone else would be travelling with me.

I remembered the *Enterprise*. The way the stately ship looked when it began to move out of Spacedock. The breaking of rules by middle-aged men who should have known better, taking her out to save their shipmate and damning the consequences.

The way life should be lived.

I set the alarm.

Now all there was to do was wait.

My Helen of Troy, for whom I stole the Enterprise

From: James Christie
Sent: 28 February 2010 20:06
To: Juliet Landau
Subject: Re Take Flight: my Gary Oldman Documentary

Dear Miss Landau

Taking flight myself in a few hours after a hair-raisingly close shave with the travel insurance – they'd post-dated it a year…

Best wishes

James

I took flight that first day of March, forcing the fear into a little box in my guts, sharpening my Asperger focus until the world was clear and stark, negotiating the terminal with a calm and steady step and once I cleared customs and departures, seeing the lines of the ship for the first time. The sky might be my sea but the ship was mine again, and as I waited in the lounge for the gate to open, the calm of a captain at the tiller came upon me.

Outcomes, options, strategy, worst-case scenarios and hopes were all calculated subconsciously – the hard focus a slack-jawed package holidaymaker does not have. Consciously, I checked passport, tickets, money and travellers' cheques every so often. The kind of seemingly obsessive-compulsive behaviour the independent traveller really needs because everything can so easily be lost on the road, and once it's lost, it's lost for good.

I also thought about an article I'd just read which cheerfully told me the odds of being killed in a plane crash. I was flying in a Boeing 757, an aircraft type which had crashed five times and had a fatal accident once in every 183 flights. There had been 38 fatal accidents involving all kinds of aircraft between 1942-2009 in the month of March, and I had a 69 percent chance of survival if I sat near the tail of the plane compared to a 51 percent chance of death if I was close to the cockpit.

Good to know!

In the film *Rain Man*, the fictional Autist Raymond Babbit might have been too scared and facts-obsessed to fly on anything but Qantas, but we are not all like him. I'd bought the ticket, accepted the risk, reminded myself that no form of transport is totally safe and told myself that if I ended up sitting next to a little old lady, not to terrorise her by quoting such reassuring statistics or suggesting we assume crash positions when the plane came in to land...

Then came the call to board, and I walked along the covered gangway.

Travelling six-and-a-half-hours in high flight and going back five in time allowed me to obey another of my travellers' rules: always arrive early, when the sun and your energy are both high. If you arrive late, the primal fear of being without shelter far from home may claim you, as it oft claimed me.

When I saw the Eastern seaboard of the United States, I knew my trip was real. While I waited in the customs and immigration hall for the officers to interview me I made my face impassive, handing my passport to the lady with economical disinterest, answering questions about my home and mortgage with the false authority of one who has nothing to hide and knowing, as she handed back the passport and I walked beneath the great sign saying WELCOME TO THE UNITED STATES OF AMERICA, that I had done it.

32

The luck of the Devil

"You've dropped your coat!"

My first moments at Newark International Airport had told me I still knew how to travel. The old brain was taking on the usual inordinate load of information as I processed options, orientated myself and searched out the best way to hop a transfer bus to Manhattan. I was coping well and not walking dyspraxically into walls.

Then I saw the package holidaymaker, barely out of the terminal and already yakking hard on her mobile, oblivious to everything around her:

"I don't understand why the signal keeps fading..."

As she yakked on, blind and deaf to the fact that she was in America where things were different, her coat slid gently off her shoulder and down to the ground. For all I knew, it had her purse, credit cards, passport and tickets in it, and she was walking on, hermetically sealed to her mobile and otherwise clueless.

Two interventions from me produced no reaction. She remained surgically attached to her toy. A final, less tactful yell forcibly reacquainted her with the facts of life and impending loss.

Disaster (or at least inconvenience) was averted. I'll bet she went home missing several items, but hopefully not in a body bag.

No way for me to behave if I wanted to make it to LA.

I checked into the Gershwin on East 27th Street, tense as hell and not looking forward to sharing a dorm. Drusilla might have liked the black, red and silk décor of the boutique hotel and would probably have eaten her bedmates before settling down to a quiet night's knitting, but I didn't really have that option. I forced myself through the shock of the new, went to bed early that night, woke even earlier the next morning and clomped down to the lobby.

New York was asleep (sometimes this happens) but I was awake. I plugged Juliet the Notebook in, smiled at Juliet Landau's picture on the desktop, and began to write:

Fear what you may find

Every man who sets out upon a search fears what he may find, for any quest requires valour in the face of unknowable trials and the cosy certainty of a happy ending can never be assured. Jay Gatsby, if I remember correctly, searched vainly to restore his version of that unsullied shore first seen by the Pilgrim Fathers. The flawed present could not easily bear comparison with the pristine past. But even though he fought manfully against the tide, time ceaselessly beat against him, sweeping him back past the outer banks and into oblivion.

I first came to New York 21 years ago, dropping exhausted from a Greyhound bus at the Port Authority Bus Terminal, searching for a happy ending after a year-long voyage around the world. I do not remember the fear, but it must have been there. New York was still wrestling with its demons of crime and corruption then so neither of us was due a hearts-and-flowers finale at the time, but I saw the city again a year or so before 9/11 – by then bright, brash, unsullied and optimistic – a Venice of the New World rising from the lagoon without a hint of gloom. After the towers fell. the headlines went around the world and the scars lay deep in the body of the metropolis, but like Gatsby, the city fought manfully against the tide, creating the New York I was seeing today.

Glasgow's airport was the first port of call along the way, and it seemed like a hybrid: half building-site, half impossibly buffed and polished customer service personnel beaming beneath hateful, hurtful fluorescent lights. The Departures hall was a

*cacophony of sound and queues and confusion where I was asked
to remove my shoes and considered dropping my pants instead.
I was lucky to even be there, if luck is the word. A late-breaking
disaster (of discovering I was about to fly without insurance) had
been averted by a last-minute miracle and the fear of that close
a call so near to zero hour stayed with me, winding and grinding
into my guts over the Atlantic. If it is down to the luck of the Devil
that I am here, then it will not surprise me if he insists on having
his pound of flesh in payment.*

*Perhaps he has been waiting for me all this time, cursing the fact I
stayed a short step ahead of him all those years ago. And perhaps
I am drawn back to see if I can outrun the odds once more. The
tremendous effort of planning this journey and of tearing myself
out of my routines has chipped away at me, and I am reminded
of my own vulnerability. Perhaps I, too, will be swept beyond the
outer banks.*

*But the city which does not sleep seems to have arisen like the
Phoenix. Wall Street and Lehman Brothers may have helped
cause the credit crunch, the US is probably over-committed in
Iraq and Afghanistan, power is flowing from West to East, and
the ordinary American in the street lives with a fear of becoming
ill that I doubt most Republicans will ever understand. Yet
Gatsby's energy continues to zing around the concrete canyons
of America's unofficial capital, and I do not see it all ending
tomorrow.*

James Christie
March 1 2010

I pressed Send and sent the first blog on its way, not knowing
that Jim was also wondering whether or not I could outrun the
odds. As he said to me later:

*"I knew what James could do, but I had reservations. A British
tourist had just been shot dead in Amarillo. He'd simply been in*

the wrong place at the wrong time. All it would take was one trip through the wrong door for James to end up the same way.

A lot of people talk and talk and you know it's never going to lead to anything. But he went out there and did it. One day we were discussing it at Morton's, the next we were in the office with articles coming in from New York, Chicago and, well, Amarillo...

In a sense, he really did steal the Enterprise, *and we helped him do it. On the second or third of March, I was walking past Carol Evans' office and she called me in. The first blogs were coming in over the Wi-Fi. We all clustered round her desk and I remember Carol saying:*

'He's done it. He's made it. He's out there again and going for LA.'

It wasn't a TV episode, a play or a film. It was real, and it was surreal."

I saw the sun was rising so I went over to a café just off 5th Avenue. It wasn't exactly a Chelsea morning, more a Manhattan sunrise, best appreciated while eating my first street-legal, US issue Hershey bar and a New York cream cheese bagel, sitting on a high-backed silver chair watching dawn break over the Empire State and listening to radio station Light FM gaily broadcast ads for hospitals, including a 'cyberknife' said to burn out tumours with great precision.

From: James Christie
Sent: 01 March 2010 16:51
To: Juliet Landau
Subject: James taking flight…

Dear Miss Landau

The Empire State Building looks very nice today, and I'm emailing from right next door to it!

How are you?

Best wishes

James

At the time, my dear Miss Landau was busy directing *Take Flight*, a documentary about the actor Gary Oldman's creative process. *And I'm busy, too,* I thought. *Flying high and getting closer. Not eight time zones away any more, but only three. Slowly getting in sync.*

The job for that day was to see the towers no longer there and to merge my memories from another century with the gritty facts of the present day. I was out of my time and place, youthful for my years and wearing the face of that other man I'd been, 20 years and a millennium-turn away. 1989 and 2000. Before the new era.

The world is a place of wonder. Over the span of human history very few people have lived from one millennium to another. The chance comes only once in a thousand years and few realise their stroke of good fortune, to live to see the page of human history turn above a shimmering blue world wreathed in cloud and smoke. Seared by plague and battle but also illuminated by love and wisdom.

The new era, such as it was, was marked not only by the turning of the calendar's page, but by the fall of the two towers. First year of the new millennium, uniquely scarred by Al Qaeda's destruction of the World Trade Center and, in a moment, the change of one world order for another. The great and grimy games of the political Cold War played out between two pragmatic superpowers had been swapped for perestroika and the fanatical uncertainties of a hot religious war fought between the only hyperpower and a thousand-headed hydra, with China waiting in the wings.

In 1989, fresh from Australia and California, I'd lain on the ground in the plaza between the Twin Towers and gazed up the vertical precipice towards the 102nd floor of the south tower, a sure way to get vertigo even when lying down on solid mother earth. Lockerbie had been fresh in my mind: I'd just passed the Pan Am Building with demonstrators freshly planted outside, wanting to know the truth about flight 103.

In 2000, I'd taken the opportunity of a weekend break in New York and, still as strong as I'd become slaving in orchards and plantations in Oz, I'd ascended the south tower of the World Trade Center in the morning and the Empire State in the evening.

I suppose there are a few thousand people left like me who can make that statement, but no-one else in human history will ever be able to say that. In so doing I became part of that history, locked in days of Cold War terrorism, an ageing frustrated spook with a few photos taken from the gantry atop the south tower and memories of breakfasting in the top-floor diner, glancing at the Lady Liberty paperweights and T-shirts in the shop, looking at the wraparound internal montage of New York's history, celebrated in word and deed. I remember a picture of James Brown, and the words, "they built this city on rock and roll." I remember standing in the footwell in front of the guardrail in the diner, my feet almost touching the floor-to-ceiling plate-glass window and half an inch from a thousand foot drop, taking pictures of Ellis Island, Liberty and the Hudson with my trusty old Zenith camera. It was pre-digital and so was I. I did not know, as I kept my balance and my nerve, that the first ripples of catastrophic change were starting virtually beneath my feet as Microsoft lost its antitrust suit against the US government, as the NASDAQ index on Wall Street started to slide and the dot.coms began to crash, denting America's global economic hegemony, perhaps fatally and forever. A financial crash prefacing the physical crash of the towers eighteen months later.

I went home to quiet desperation while the world went to war in anger, spinning into a science-fiction future mixed with the tragic repetition of past mistakes. The Fall of Sunnydale was nothing compared to the Fall of the Towers. Empires in all but name, locked in intractable struggle in Afghanistan and Iraq. To a generation (*my* generation) born in the days of Apollo 11, the first colour televisions, Marc Bolan's glam rock and the three-day week, the year 2001 had seemed as far away and alien as a space odyssey; and once myself and my compatriots had lived that far into the future it would have seemed only natural for us to fade out and make way for the next generation. The new frontiersmen who spoke the language of Windows and Apple, and lived through Facebook and Twitter.

Yet geeks throughout the ages had often dreamed of time machines. Of doors which let the lucky traveller, still young, walk out into a different summer and another day.

I was that lucky traveller, a middle-aged man kidding himself with dreams of youth. But there was a twist to my tale, and a reminder that some truths are stranger than fiction. A few days before I left Glasgow, I'd been at the Autism Resource Centre in Maryhill on another errand and fallen into conversation with the Information Officer.

As well as being really pleased about it, I had always been curious as to why my hair had never greyed, my face remained relatively unlined and (despite a two year layoff) why my body had responded to the brutal workouts I put it through at the Kelvin like that of a 28-year-old. The day after my first gym session I'd had an early morning meeting with Jim at the NAS in Hope Street. Not unreasonably, I had expected to turn up exhausted, crocked and in agony.

In fact, despite scarcely bothering to warm up and putting my hands into hundreds of head-on collisions with heavy bags, I woke up with one little twinge, just one, in my right shoulder.

"We've got a lot of young-looking people round here," the Information Officer said. "Seems a lot of people on the spectrum also have the Peter Pan gene."

Peter Pan. The boy who never grew up.

"Really?"

"Yes. It looks like most Autists lack copies of a certain gene sequence which speeds up ageing. In addition, they – you – have longer than average telomeres."

"Telomeres?"

"Yeah, little safety caps stuck on the ends of your chromosomes. They protect the DNA molecules *inside* the chromosomes, which hold the body's blueprints. So the longer the telomeres, the more slowly your biological clock ticks. That's because the DNA, which has been protected by the telomeres and is therefore undamaged, can go on giving the cells a *proper* guide to follow in order to return you to your factory specs if you're ageing or you've been injured."

"What, I regenerate like Doctor Who? You're kidding."

"Not quite. Every time your DNA is used as a guide to restore you, a bit gets clipped off the end of the telomere. But then there's an enzyme called telomerase – which you may also have – which repairs the telomere itself. No one lives forever, but the longer the telomere keeps the DNA safe and the more telomerase there is to fix the telomere, the longer you'll stay young."

The world was indeed a place of wonder.

I showered, prepared to walk the 25 or so blocks to Ground Zero, and looked at my face in the mirror. The smooth skin and blond hair, much the same as it had been in 1989. The Information Officer in Maryhill had stressed that the telomere theory hadn't been verified yet, but it answered a lot of questions for me.

Autism wasn't a handicap. It also had advantages.

It had enabled me to walk through time's door into that other summer and see the world with a young man's eyes. A gift beyond price.

I walked down through the streets of Manhattan, and when I'd seen what had become of the towers I went down to the

Esplanade and looked across at Jersey. I noticed a young mother with a baby-buggy out of the corner of my eye as I opened my Pukka Pad and started writing:

Ground Zero, afterwards

There's always a girl sitting alone on a bench. Work goes on to put up a new building in place of the lost towers, and the sound of the ta-pocketa ta-pocketa *machines reverberate above the din. The skeleton of the new edifice rises from the foundations. Raw-red girders are just beginning to climb skyward, but she's always there.*

I cross the causeway to West Street and Battery Park. A young man brushes by me on the escalator, wrapped tight in his own private little world of finance and shutting out all else with headphones. I met another young man like him once, in the plaza before the towers fell.

I come to the water's edge and relative silence greets me. There's Lady Liberty in the distance and closer, Ellis Island. I saw them from a higher vantage point before.

I remember this borough is an island. Quite a fragile little sliver, really. The people never really thought the terror could reach them, but it did.

The young girl sits on the bench. She has her thoughts on other matters, perhaps, and it is a cold and chilly day, but it is as if she is a witness, reminding those who remain of life's vulnerability and of its beauty.

The branches of the trees, not yet clothed in leaves, are stark against the sky. A young mother pushing a baby-buggy walks past. The occasional jogger passes by. Youngsters throw snowballs. People still smile.

James Christie
March 2 2010

It seemed like a good piece of work. I'd have to show it to Miss L– ...

Not Miss Landau. Juliet. I'd have to show it to Juliet.

33

Noo Yawk

From: Christie, James
Sent: 03 March 2010 16:41
To: Keith Erskine
Subject: Greyhound to Chicago

Hi Keith

Just consulted the Greyhound website, and I have the mildly ghastly option of taking the 12.50 pm on Friday from DC and arriving in the windy city at 4.55 am. I've done this before and am quite sanguine about the 17-hour grind, so I'll get in, breakfast in a diner and then take a taxi to Randolph Street to arrive at a slightly less unearthly hour. Hope this is all right.

Best wishes

James

From: Keith Erskine
Sent: 03 March 2010 16:49
To: Christie, James
Subject: RE: Greyhound to Chicago

Hi James

Jings! That's quite a journey. You're welcome here any time James, so please don't feel you've got to kill yourself to make it for the weekend. If you want to arrive later on Saturday, Sunday or even next week, that's fine too.

Regards,

Keith

From: Christie, James
Sent: 03 March 2010 16:58
To: Keith Erskine
Subject: RE: Greyhound to Chicago

Hi Keith

Need to make progress as my friend in California may be going to UK soon, so I think I'll have to be a bit of a masochist. Don't worry, it won't kill me. Probably.

Regards

James

From: Keith Erskine
Sent: 03 March 2010 16:49
To: Christie, James
Subject: RE: Greyhound to Chicago

OK James, the life of a traveler!

Regards,

Keith

Most people think they take the trip. It ain't so. The trip takes them. Earlier hopes of seeing Philadelphia and Gettysburg were dashed in favour of getting straight to Washington DC and from there to Chicago, running for Los Angeles to stay ahead of Miss Landau's date in Cyprus.

It would be the worst of times were I to arrive in LA just one day late and miss her.

I checked out of the Gershwin on the morning of March 3, walked up 8th Avenue to the Port Authority Bus Terminal on 42nd Street, and tried to ignore the growing cacophony of sound coming from Times Square. This was the heart of one America – a brawling, brash, beautiful city with its face of gold and its heart black as pitch, crossroads of a New World and beacon of hope summoning the Old. Its inhabitants running themselves off their feet in search of a new Jerusalem sandwiched between blood-red adverts for Coca-Cola, or just lookin' to see where it was all happenin' amidst skyscrapers of silver and glass, outposts of neon and the babble of many tongues in its towers of Babel. Manhattan, sold to the white man in 1626 for goods worth 60 guilders.

It really was deafening.

Autists can be overloaded by too much light and sound. Some wouldn't last a minute in Times Square. I had more resistance than most, but it felt like taking a subtle battering from a skilled puncher and I didn't particularly wish to hang around the arteries of the Square too long.

I got my wish. The second – the very *second* – I pushed through one of the multiple doors into the bus terminal, I passed from the brash America of Noo Yawk into that other place often called the 'real' America by tourists.

The décor, in contrast to the smorgasbord of sound and technicolour outside, was muted green and faded brown. Every single one of the staff was black and the passengers mainly poor. Above all, it was quiet. I've been in arid regions with scarcely a living soul for miles which weren't that quiet. God knows how thick the walls of that terminal were (perhaps it had been built in the 50s and designed to double as a nuclear bunker in case 'Them Darn Russkies Dropped The Big One,' as a hawkish general of the time might have said) but if I'd been dropped there blindfolded I might have been persuaded I was on Rannoch Moor.

I took the voucher I had been sent and prepared to swap it for the Greyhound Discovery Pass. Proffering vouchers seemed a little bit unreal and stressful. I was used to going to travel agents and receiving paper tickets, not booking online and getting vouchers I had to print out myself. Young face or not, I was from another time and I half-expected the clerk to look at

Washington from Lincoln

me in a funny way and ask what the *hay*-ell this stupid piece of paper was. I didn't have the neuro-typical wiring which would have allowed me the luxury of assuming everything would be all right.

Most Autists have much higher levels of fear and anxiety because of our different mindset. The facts in front of me were black and white, and I couldn't kid myself about them one iota. Either my silly voucher would be accepted and exchanged for a bus pass opening up America to me or it wouldn't, and I'd had to sweat and wait three months to find out what would happen.

For an Autist, every day is an exercise in overcoming stress and anxiety, often about seemingly trivial matters. The only way for us to beat the devils which ride us is to exert rational thought and apply coping strategies.

So, like a thinner than average Terminator, I stood sullenly before the clerk, painstakingly working out the options, trying to look relaxed, and awaiting the verdict.

It only took a moment. She tapped something into her machine and I had my bus pass. America was open. Right now, I would be going to an HI Hostel on 10th Street in Washington DC and I'd been able to book a bed ahead with Juliet's help.

Juliet the Notebook, of course. The real Juliet was still a long way away.

Sometimes, though, it felt like she was right by my side, much as Drusilla had been; and if it seemed she commanded me to go on, then that was what I would do:

The Endurance or Erosion of Equality

"... a new nation conceived in liberty and dedicated
to the proposition that all men are created equal."

(Abraham Lincoln)

The words on the sign overlooking the interstate on the way out of New York stood out with bleak, efficient clarity:

DIVORCE $399

Phone 1-800-ambulance-chasing lawyer

The Port Authority Bus Terminal had been both a calming but downbeat opposite to New York's frenetic and colourful energy, and a clear reminder that this was the way the poor folks in America travelled. A man with the face and voice of a disappointed Morgan Freeman was at the wheel of the Greyhound bus. He scarcely said a thing for the whole four hour trip to Washington DC, but his face lit up in surprise when I thanked him for delivering me safely.

A black man aggressively tried to panhandle change from me outside a 7-11 at Silver Spring on the outskirts of DC, a Muslim taxi-driver helped me avoid being conned by an unlicensed cabbie outside the Washington terminal, a gay man at the youth hostel assured me Americans were still liberal in person, and a park ranger at the Lincoln Memorial admitted he feared the ideals of liberty and equality upon which America was founded may well be eroding.

With the host of problems facing today's America, it is not hard to see why the soulless dissolution of a romantic ideal, the disappointment of a life's promise, the driven aggression of a man locked in poverty and the desperate cons being practised by those on the edge can be experienced so easily. Abraham Lincoln's America was tested as never before in the fires of the Civil War, and although the guns of Shiloh are silent now, and the men who fought at Valley Forge in their bare feet are gone, the tests of his nation's endurance go implacably on.

It was good to hear that gay rights were being respected, and reassuring that people still remember Lincoln's words well enough to fear that their echo may be becoming weaker. Lincoln himself wondered "whether that nation or any nation so conceived and so dedicated can long endure."

One might wonder what decisions Lincoln would take if he was in office today. He would surely still stand resolutely for equality, but would he have opted for isolationism or involved America more deeply in foreign affairs? Perhaps Lincoln's greatest asset was his integrity, for he did not hesitate to make hard choices in the hardest of times.

If Barack Obama wishes truly to change America, he must be willing to forsake that which he has sought and make decisions which will most likely deny him a second term in office. Every weak decision made since Abraham Lincoln's day has eroded his ideals, and the possibility that government of the people by the people for the people shall *perish has increased.*

I could finish on that note but instead I'll mention that last night, less than spitting distance away from the marbled halls of the White House, I saw a homeless white man sleeping rough outside a branch of Borders. Examples of poverty like this have been used so often that they have descended into cliché, but I doubt the man in question was much concerned about that. He was probably just hoping to make it through the night without freezing, being kicked in the ribs, or worse

James Christie
March 4 2010

34

Chicago blues

From: James Christie
Sent: 04 March 2010 11:52
To: Juliet Landau
Subject: Servers and mighty rivers…

Dear Miss Landau

Sorry to hear your server's on the fritz again. Better mention that after seeing the Lincoln Memorial, I will yank myself west on Friday with a 17 hour Greyhound trip to Chicago, weekend at my cousin's there and, depending on time, either ford mighty rivers, tramp across great plains and crawl west through sagebrush on the 8th, or more prosaically take the bus or even hop an internal flight to LA if time is shorter than short…

Take care

Best wishes

James

From: Juliet Landau
Sent: 04 March 2010 17:26
To: James Christie
Subject: Servers and mighty rivers…

Have a nice time with your cousin!

Juliet

"This is the *capital* of the *world*!" the Muslim taxi-driver said to me as we sped from the seedy Greyhound stop to the HI Hostel. It can be extremely difficult getting one's orientation on arrival in a strange city and, once again, Autists are pretty bad at it.

What brave and sophisticated method did I pull out of my bag of tricks to overcome this latest obstacle?

A very simple one.

I cheated. I took a cab. I had a bit more money than I had had 20 years before so I side-slipped a potential source of stress and got a chauffeur-driven trip to the door. Admittedly, I nearly got conned by an unlicensed cabbie before finding my Muslim friend, but my experience came to my aid and I avoided a round-about trip charge of 40 dollars, paying a reasonable rate of 10 dollars instead.

The hostel was superbly tidy (perhaps their cleaners were on the spectrum?), the guests with whom I was sharing dorm-space wonderfully polite (an American characteristic I tend to like after a few too many years' experience of West of Scotland violence) and Wi-Fi access easy and efficient. I'd said several times before I left that all my equipment absolutely positively had to work reliably. My old Zenith camera was built like a Russian T-34 tank and had the reliability of an AK-47. It wasn't the lightest or fastest piece of photographic machinery around, and with a 58mm lens, I'd often had to back up half-a-mile or so to capture all of the image in the viewfinder, but it never, ever failed to deliver and that was what counted on the road.

"I can't call the bloody Microsoft helpline if I'm in a foxhole somewhere getting shelled!" I'd said to Jim back in Hope Street. Jim patiently explained to me that I was going to America, not Afghanistan. I'd grumbled that parts of America were *like* Afghanistan, but now I was here and about the only thing the hostel lacked was a bar serving martinis.

Nevertheless, there was a sense of the spiderweb delicately shaking. I'd bought a padlock at the hostel, forgotten to use it and left the contents of my locker free to be pilfered, but I'd been lucky and those around me honest. Every traveller usually makes a mistake in the first week as the rust comes off. This was mine, but I'd weathered it.

Then I'd read Juliet's tweets on Twitter, heard she was having server/host problems and felt a stab of alarm. Email was our main method of communication. Without it I might reach LA but be unable to find her when I got there.

Well, what had an old friend said to me?

What's for you won't go by you..."

I would go across America then, and put that saying to the test:

A Yank towards Chicago

While a gay black dancer (who admitted he fancied me) and a white construction worker from the Midwest made plans to attend the ballet together, I found out (courtesy of Street Sense, *Washington DC's version of* The Big Issue*) that Mayor Fenty of DC recently decided* "to disallow any more homeless people into shelters" *although* "there are 7,000 homeless individuals in DC and 2,400 beds available."

Thank you from the bottom of my heart, Mayor Fenty, and I hope you freeze slowly to death on the street, although your heart is surely stone-cold dead already.

I made my way to DC's Greyhound terminal, noting how quickly the sidewalks deteriorated once I was beyond the marbled triangle of Lincoln Memorial, White House and Capitol Hill.

There was no boarding call for the bus to Chicago, but the staff hung around with sniffer dogs, the pile of bags lined up before the gate and after we waited a languid little while, it seemed we really ought to go.

A friendly Alsatian sniffed me up and down, a bored guy called Levi Billups bunged my bag in the baggage hold, and inside the bus a black lady in a grey tracksuit complained soulfully into her cell phone that:

"...*ah* have been *dis*respected. If ah'd have been a white woman he wouldn't have talked to me like *that*..."

Though angry, her voice still had the smoky rhythm of Chicago blues.

Then the bus began to move, and for one fleeting moment I felt that sense of freedom for which all travellers live. My heart was light with expectation, my mind calm and clear. It was 20 years since I had travelled, and it was as if I had never been away.

I was yanking myself clear of the Eastern seaboard and far into the west, and I didn't have much time, but I felt alive.

I imagined I could hear Drusilla's voice, softly singing Scarborough Fair *as the bus climbed past the northern spurs of the Alleghenies on route 915, heading for Pittsburgh on roads studded with hideous outposts composed of Starbucks, McDonalds and motels, all festooned with heavy-duty cabling strung around great tall masts advertising the available wares. In contrast, though, picturesque timber-frame houses, long rectangular barns and tall feed-silos dotted the fir and pine-clad ridges as the bus breasted the summit and headed down towards Steel City.*

We changed buses in Pittsburgh, and I sweated through my autistic dislike of enforced change, dispassionately observing my own fear as I willed myself to concentrate on the procedure of disembarking, claiming my luggage and reboarding. Get it wrong, boy, *I thought,* and you're staying in Pittsburgh. *The rules of travel are not forgiving of carelessness or panic.*

We changed again in Cleveland and I got into Chicago at 5 am on a cold March morning, icily willing the panic down again as I orientated myself and found the way to my cousin's apartment on Randolph Street. Most Aspergers struggle through the day like climbers hanging on to a rope. For an Autist, getting through an ordinary day is like jogging up a small hill: it takes an effort, but at least the routine is familiar and support is nearby. For this Asperger, getting to Chicago along the unknown roads of a foreign country was like climbing K2, but now I'd reached the summit of the escarpment. All I had to do next was take the long road down into America's heartland and reach Los Angeles.

Sounds simple, doesn't it?

Trust me, it isn't.

Hell, Dru, where are you?

James Christie

March 9 2010

As the bus pulled into Chicago, I saw a poster of Julianna Margulies. She was starring in *The Good Wife*, a hit legal drama set in the second city.

Shc looked a bit like Juliet.

I also remember something else, way up in the Alleghenies on the Interstate, thinking, musing and looking back down a long valley spruced up with pines. Seeing a great white church in the distance, boxy and stark.

To pass the long hours, travellers sometimes fall into a contemplative state. The mind seems to empty and truths become apparent. I don't know how it works.

All I do know is that a single thought came to me, and though I am loath to believe in fate, I cannot forget its words:

I'm going to my destiny.

Some ways of reaching your destiny are more striking than others. Stopping at Somerset, Pennsylvania

35

2,048 miles to go

"**Y**ou look about all in."

The black concierge at my cousin Keith's apartment building on Randolph Street was friendly, and certainly perceptive. The sun had just come up, Lake Michigan was to my right and Macy's behind me. I might have looked like hell, but despite being fully laden I'd walked over Chicago's bridges and under the El (elevated railroad) without a twinge or complaint right after a 17-hour journey from the Eastern seaboard. It seemed the Peter Pan gene was alive and working well.

The weekend passed in a whirl of sight and sound blow-dried and sharpened by the wind. The view over both America and Canada from the 1,127-foot John Hancock Tower, a vista of skyscrapers on Lakeshore Drive which would not have looked out of place in *Blade Runner*, the hospitality (and the blessed

Atop the escarpment, ready to take the long, low road to LA

use of washing machine and tumble dryer) from Keith – but my thoughts ever-turning towards the long way still to go.

A picture taken by Keith at the Ferris Wheel on the pier just off Lakeshore Drive summed it up. There was one of those tourist signs, giving distances from Chicago to other famous cities. Paris 4153 miles, Delhi 7484 miles...

And Los Angeles. 1745 miles.

I stood in front of the sign and pointed west, feeling dour. I would not fly fleet above those many miles but cover them by bus, one by one. In fact, according to my old Rand McNally map, it was even further: 2,048 miles. Probably the distance by road as opposed to a straight-line calculation.

It was wet, I was tired and time was against me. I was running for Los Angeles and there was a real chance I could arrive only hours too late.

Lake Michigan was choppy and the weather cold, but that was no excuse to stop or even slow. No real experience ever came cheap, and if I had to suffer a little more on account of my autism, then that was part of the deal.

Run for Los Angeles then, as hard and fast as I could! I would ride the bus into the Great Plains on the morning of March 8 and go as far as Amarillo, deep in the Texas Panhandle – a 23-hour stint which I judged was as much as I could take. At the time, I had completely forgotten Jim's mention of the British tourist shot dead in Amarillo but it probably wouldn't have changed my decision. America aspired to be the land of opportunity and the opportunity to get killed was equally available in any US city.

If there should be a calm before the storm, in which the knight could consider the trials the next day would set him, such calm was mine that early Sunday morn. Alone in the white and glassy lounge on the 27th floor, watched benignly by Ceres, goddess of agriculture (her statue was on top of the nearby Chicago Board of Trade Building), and illuminated by the surrounding towers' strong and steady glow, I finished my latest blog on Juliet the Notebook, thought of Juliet the Landau, and looked up some poetry to quote to her:

From: James Christie
Sent: 07 March 2010 00:55
To: Juliet Landau
Subject: Re: Amid the alien corn…

Dear Miss Landau

Late on at my cousin's apartment after a very tiring couple of days, but wondered how you were and found myself thinking of Keats for no particular reason:

> … amid the alien corn;
> The same that oft-times hath
> Charmed magic casements, opening on the foam
> Of perilous seas, in faery lands forlorn.

Perhaps the kind of words sailors read, far from shore in the long hours of the off-watches, or travellers, setting out into the Great Plains long ago.

Best wishes

James

The night was velvet, the moment perfect.

I clicked on Send and the email didn't go.

I checked Twitter and found the truth. Juliet's server/host had gone down. I couldn't get through.

1,745 miles or more to go, and now I was flying blind. Nor did I know how well or otherwise my articles were doing on the NAS Facebook page, but Carol Evans later told me how she felt as the articles came in to Hope Street from points further and further West:

"When I read James' words as they arrived from the US, I was transported to hot and dusty streets, echoing bus stations, noise-filled highways and every location in between. I felt James' anticipation, his anxiety, his heartfelt desire to fulfil his dream and meet Miss Landau. This was an epic journey for a man with Aspergers. Such a journey would change his life and people's

perceptions about Asperger Syndrome. It certainly changed mine. James ventured into the unknown on a daily basis with very few resources. His own motivation, determination and passion kept him going. To the onlooker, the possibility of failure was very high yet James never gave up.

I felt privileged to be part of the journey, and who could not be impressed? How many others would take such a risk with their security, their confidence and their heart?"

(Carol Evans, former Director of the NAS
in Scotland and Northern Ireland)

Shagged out in Chicago, and still so far to go...

36

Turning into Homer Simpson

Know the way to Amarillo?

*I*n order to find my way to Amarillo, I'd be changing from service 1315 to service 1353 at St Louis, while the first bus would be going on to Los Angeles via Kansas City, Denver and Las Vegas. It was the first time I had seen the name of my final destination on the front of a bus, but I still had over 2,000 miles and two time zones to go.

It would take me nearly a full day of non-stop travel to reach Amarillo, the town's elegiac name picked off the map as the farthest I could get from Chicago towards LA in one go before the desperate need for sleep overcame me.

Of all things, a line from Rocky IV kept going through my head as I waited for departure:

"Mighty long way, baby!"

Rocky's trainer was advising him he was in for a long, bruising fight against Ivan Drago, that the fight was probably going to go the distance. I only had a long distance to travel, but I felt a bit like an aging heavyweight boxer trudging into a lengthy contest.

I once saw a scene in an old film, where a group of soldiers were being sent out to die at the behest of their general. They were drinking their last night away in a tavern, and they made the serving girl sing. Her voice was sweet as a thorn bird, and the men fell silent and listened.

I hear the song of a sweet voice and soft come the words of Scarborough Fair, so I pick up my rucksack and trudge over to gate 18. The Greyhound should be there but they've gone and parked it at gate 19 instead. I must make sure I board the right bus. There is no one to correct my mistakes for me. My Greyhound pass is non-refundable. If I lose it, it's gone. Simple as that.

I manage to find my place and the long journey into the heart of America begins as the bus cruises south along Interstate 55. This is the successor to the legendary Route 66, the road ex-GIs with their young families took to Los Angeles after World War Two in search of olive groves, celebrity and the American Dream.

The brown and surly fields slowly begin to glint with the gold of wheat, and the last snow in the roadside gullies fades away. There is a glimmer of America's golden age in the memory of the land. Of bobby-soxers, bubblegum and baseball games. But then I see a large sign for an adult superstore and remember that the gilded age of Eisenhower's America is long gone.

As the bus moves ever-so-slowly south amidst the immensity of plain and corn, the country feels like a grumpy, middle-aged patient slowly shrugging off a heavy chest cold and vulnerable to a relapse as it struggles out of the depression.

We stop in Springfield, Illinois, and I have a sudden vision of a giant Homer Simpson looming over the plains. There really is a building nearby which, flanked as it is by smokestacks, looks strangely similar to Mr Burns' nuclear power plant. On closer inspection it turns out to be a multi-storey Crowne Plaza hotel built in front of a factory.

St Louis comes and goes, or at least it would have if the bus to which I am supposed to transfer had turned up on time. Instead, myself and several dozen disgruntled Americans stand around in line feeling our veins turning varicose and wondering if we will remain lost in Missouri forever.

With a land area of 3.79 million square miles, much of it relatively empty by British standards, getting across America takes a long time. As the Greyhound heads south, traces of red earth appear and west of Elk City, Oklahoma, I see my first piece of tumbleweed skittering across the freeway.

Amarillo itself, deep in the Texas Panhandle, has suffered the fate of many small American towns. The shops and businesses in the town centre have relocated to the outskirts, clustering around the freeway on-ramps and exits, leaving the old main street empty and lifeless. Fittingly, the first billboard I see when

I arrive is offering cheap funerals: $895 for a straight cremation or $3,795 for the full works.

I make the daft decision to walk to my motel on the outskirts, nearly lose my way, see firsthand evidence that Texas freight trains really can be a mile long when I end up in a freight yard, and get a fine case of sunburn and blisters into the bargain. Experience gets me through, and when I eat at a local restaurant that night the waitress, who sports a fine set of mismatched teeth, is amazed that I have walked. No-one walks to motels in America. There may even be a law against it. I have probably earned myself a place in the record books, or perhaps I am merely turning into Homer Simpson.

I catch up on my sleep at the motel, take the bus back into town in the morning and hang around the Greyhound depot for an extra couple of hours when the service to Albuquerque is late. I fret and get angry, the Americans shrug their shoulders phlegmatically, and I begin to realise that the assumptions many make about them are largely wrong. The brash American does exist, but it seems he is confined to Capitol Hill. A cartoon in the Amarillo Independent *(a free newspaper) depicts a rebellious crowd protesting outside the White House, demanding the leadership do something while the politicians cower inside, reluctant to take action.*

But in real life, no one is protesting outside the White House. Perhaps it is time for Americans to embrace their own stereotypes, get angry and rebel.

Rebel against what?

I don't know, but as Marlon Brando once said, whaddya got?

James Christie

March 14 2010

From: James Christie
Sent: 09 March 2010 15:33
To: Juliet Landau
Cc: James Doherty
Subject: Re: Servers and mighty rivers…

Dear Miss Landau

Emailing more than usual as I understand your server's down, and I am therefore coming in blindly on a wing and a prayer. 24 hours in a Greyhound bus from Chicago to Amarillo, and I'm not even any relation to Tony Christie, or Julie Christie, come to think of it.

Oh, well. Planning on being in Hollywood for 5 nights from Friday 12th inclusive, which I hope to God will be in time.

No Wi-Fi in my Motel 6, so thanks also to God for my friendly neighbourhood Starbucks.

Hope to hell this gets through.

Best wishes

James

No answer.

Keep going.

I turned back to Juliet the Notebook, painstakingly made my brain work out when I should expect to arrive in LA. *Go for Albuquerque and Las Vegas,* I thought. *Forget the Grand Canyon – Juliet's worth more than a hole in the ground – and book one night in Albuquerque, two in Vegas and five in LA.*

I brought out my credit card, prayed it wouldn't be cancelled, and accessed the appropriate websites.

153

From: James Christie
Sent: 09 March 2010 16:16
To: Juliet Landau
Cc: James Doherty
Subject: Schrader Boulevard

Dear Miss Landau

Well, committed now, or perhaps I need to be! At the USA Hostel Hollywood on 1624 Schrader Boulevard for five nights 12th-16th March.

Hope to see you.

Best wishes

James

I sent off the email, wondering if I was waving in the dark, shut down Juliet the Notebook and stood up from my seat in Starbucks. My head was buzzing from the effort of planning, my feet hurt from the hike out to the Motel 6, and I wondered if I (unlike Gatsby) would find the green light, the orgastic future receding before me, or be borne back ceaselessly into the past.

I watched the cars race by on Interstate 40 for a while, then walked over to the motel.

Republican and Democrat in agreement

Jack was an old, affable Republican. Very far to the right, ex-army and ex-trucker. He was no fan of liberals or of Obama, and was God-fearing to the core. He was clear that most of America was also pretty far to the right, and he defended his right to bear arms. He smoked long cigars, ate eight slices of bacon for breakfast most mornings, and carried a battered copy of the Declaration of Independence with him everywhere.

But he wasn't truculent, and he was willing to listen and debate. He accepted improvements in healthcare had to be made ('we can't even cross state lines to get a better deal on health insurance, and that's wrong!*'), and he believed in rights for homosexuals, agreeing strongly with Lincoln that all men were created equal.*

I liked him a lot, and the five-hour bus trip from Amarillo to Albuquerque went by pretty easily. I said goodbye to Jack in Albuquerque and we wished each other a good day. I spent the night at a laid-back hostel on 10th Street where I met Don, gentle-voiced and Democrat to the core.

For his part, Don thought Congress was completely out of touch with the American people (Jack would probably have agreed) and when I commented that I wasn't seeing much of the bright optimism usually associated with Americans, he explained that everyone he had talked to was feeling very negative – a trait I usually associate with Britain.

The last few years have not been kind to the ordinary American – 9/11, service in Iraq, soaring national debt, the failed Bush administration, the credit crunch which led to millions of foreclosures on homes, and the heightening cost of healthcare premiums.

Then had come Obama, and the hope that, in the words of the song which launched Tony Blair's government, "things can only get better."

But all too soon, it seemed the peaks of overly-high expectations were replaced by deepening ravines of disappointment. The national debt could not be paid off overnight, nor could healthcare reform happen in a day.

It is as if, after a long night out on the sparkling tiles of hope, America has woken up with the biggest hangover of all time.

Jack and Don would probably both have agreed that Obama is not Superman, but America needs either to find such a man and put him (or her) at the helm, or rediscover its own spirit of optimism.

They have settled the American West, but perhaps this is their new frontier.

James Christie

March 13 2010

Coming in on a wing and a prayer

There's no safe way to take a risk. A strange tangle of interlocking events, combined with my own foolhardy drive, had brought me to Albuquerque, New Mexico, on a cold March evening.

There was Drusilla's Roses, *a story based on* Buffy the Vampire Slayer *which I casually wrote last year and which became a passion.*

There was the hankering to see the California locations I used in Roses – *Candlewood Drive in Los Angeles and Point Lobos State Reserve near Carmel – and the fear that I might never be able to do so.*

Then there was the kindness of Juliet Landau who read Roses *and complimented it, and the email correspondence which evolved from there.*

And finally, there was the subtle shift of emphasis as I began to think less of the locations and more about possibly meeting Miss Landau.

But there was always the knowledge that hope is the most fragile of things, and that something could easily go wrong. And something has gone wrong. Juliet's server is down. Apart from snail-mail I have no other way to contact her, but the only way to go is onward.

Some may say it is better to travel hopefully than to arrive, but I think I'll tell those who say that to go to hell. I will go on to Los

Angeles, I will walk the streets of Hollywood, and I will hope.

I feel a bit like the pilot of a World War Two B-17 bomber, nursing his Flying Fortress home after a mission and coming in on a wing and a prayer.

I'm flying blind myself, and I do not know what is to come.

James Christie

March 13 2010

I'd talked to Jack and Don, found out Albuquerque was a mile high and cold, been panhandled again by a mild-mannered black man on the way to the comfy easygoing hostel on 10th Street; and now, late in the evening, in a study embroidered with Indian blankets and decorated with old paperbacks, hooked Juliet the Notebook up to the hostel's Wi-Fi and searched for Juliet Landau.

Nothing.

I didn't sleep well that night.

37

Following in Steinbeck's footsteps

I headed out again, going for Vegas via Flagstaff on a white Greyhound bus, sitting with a little old lady of Chinese descent, talking to a man the spitting image of Dennis Hopper who thought I was, "like, something out of the movies, man."

I wrote as I went, as we passed through weigh stations and moved across the high desert plains like a centipede, a Pukka Pad in my hands, like the one in which I'd first written *Drusilla's Roses*. That other Rose ahead, still far ahead in Los Angeles, but here and now the words spooling out upon the paper with an ease which 'Dennis Hopper' likened to poetry in motion.

In the articles I sent back to the NAS, I sometimes talked of Drusilla as if she were there with me. She was not, but just now and then I would catch the tiniest glimpse of her, always serene and supportive, telling me it would be all right if only I could go on a little longer.

I remembered Steinbeck's tales with the clarity of a waking dream, knowing I was travelling in the wake of Jody's grandfather, who'd led the people across the great plains, and the Joads, making the crossing to California from the Oklahoma dustbowl, dry and spitting dust all the way. Though I sat safe in an air-conditioned bus in another era, I knew how they felt, with their goal of westering to the land of milk and honey.

Never enough time to beat the Cyprus deadline, but – insane as it was – I found myself wishing I could take *more* time. Find a van like Steinbeck's *Rocinante*, a dog like Charley to travel with, and take time to cross the desert, time to feel the westering in my soul like men of other days had done, brewing up by the side of the road using my old billy and thinking, ever thinking of the golden city just over the horizon.

Westering song

Travel always takes everything you've got. The fatigue crawls through my limbs like slow-moving rust, and I am weary to the bone. But I feel the call of the West, I see Old Glory fluttering on a hill above the Interstate, and I get up and go on.

John Steinbeck once wrote of an old man who led his people across the plains to the ocean, and when he got there he knew he was done. Ever after, he told his children and his children's children of the way Indians tried to steal their horses. Of how they corralled the wagons into a circle and drove them off. He told the stories so often it seemed as if the words were carved deep into worn old stone. No-one listened any more and no-one cared.

Then one day, he told his grandson what it had really been like. It hadn't been about the Indians, it hadn't been about the trail, it hadn't been about the hardship and the snakes and the high plateaus in the distance, it had only been about the westering. The long line of horses, covered wagons and settlers inching their way across the dry and stubborn land, where the shadows beneath the branches of the petrified trees were as pure black as the sun was scalding white. Burying their dead in rocky graves and moving ever onwards, until they came down to the sea and it was done.

The country grew up behind them. Desert stops became towns, towns became cities, dirt roads became highways and Tom Mix sang his way onto early TV screens. The people lost the way of westering and listened to old men's stories no more.

But it all happened not so long before living memory. Wyatt Earp died in 1929, and a man living today could have been dandled on his knee as a baby, perhaps out on the porch in Tombstone one hot afternoon in the last days of the Old West.

We so easily forget the past was real. That the faded black and white pictures were taken of scenes raw with living colour. We do not realise the old were once the young.

James Christie
March 13 2010

The Greyhound bus came into Flagstaff, where I would change for Las Vegas, late in the afternoon.

One time zone away, just one, from California.

For the first time, I saw a road sign with the words Los Angeles on it, and felt a subtle thrill, knowing I was getting close. I drank tea in a Dairy Queen with the Chinese lady, who had decided to put her faith in the Lord, wait nine hours for another connection and see where it took her.

I gazed awhile at the San Francisco Peaks, then rode the bus on up to Las Vegas. Four or five hours more across Arizona's ice-capped mountain territory, the sharp peaks melting and dissolving into high and dry red plains, heading on up to a city which spread out across the desert like a fallen star.

There was the occasional rest stop, a welcome break from the loos at the back of Greyhound buses where the wary traveller had to keep his balance as best he could and pee into a sloshing bowl of greenish disinfectant just beneath the toilet seat, and a better design than the tired old Depression-era roadside diners with a couple of faded petrol pumps out the front, fly-screened windows and no air conditioning.

An old man from Mexico sat next to me and talked of his ranch south of the border. I couldn't make out most of his words, so I watched the road as we bridged canyons and passed the odd casino, moving closer to Vegas.

Physically, I was like stone, neither tiring nor weakening nor ageing. But fear, my insidious mistress, was still with me and would not loose its grip even as we passed the Vegas city limits, the outriders of the star. Hotels and motels on the freeway's verge, hustling and bustling for trade and begging for our custom.

I got off the bus on Fremont Street, logic already beating down fear as I forcibly orientated myself and worked out which way to walk. Thirteen blocks along Fremont Street to the USA Hostel Las Vegas, but the fluorescent neon of the covered Fremont Street Experience was giving me a foretaste of a sensory overload ten times as bad as the one I'd walked

Las Vegas: halfway between the Strip and Skid Row ...

through in Times Square, and I was already mentally wearied from a 12-hour day travelling across three states.

That night and day was the test. Every brain has its hardware and its software. The software holds the higher intellectual capacity for flexibility and creativity. The hardware is the uglier, no-nonsense part of the machine which comes into play when the higher functions, either from fatigue, a hammer blow to the head, or both, no longer function.

Skills deep as bone. Burnt into me in Australia, the back-up capability to make the right decision when I couldn't think straight. Empowering me to walk through the glaring light directly to the door of the hostel, all the while logging landmarks en route, noting the casinos on the Strip far to the right, assessing potential threats as the last of the dimly lit cocktail bars on Fremont Street gave way to standard-issue American poverty, with the inevitable chain-link fences and stores accepting food stamps within sight of the Strip. Proof that history was circular and the Steinbeck-era Depression was coming around again.

If you're alone and in a rough neighbourhood, do not make eye contact. You do not know who has a knife, gun, bad attitude or all three. Especially in America, where there are at least two hundred million guns in circulation and it only takes one bullet to kill you. The distance between life and death is the distance between thumb and forefinger. One simultaneous twitch of those two fingers is all it takes to fire a gun.

I was six feet four and two hundred pounds, but I passed a couple of guys who were six feet six and two hundred and *fifty* pounds. The second guy said hi and gave me a cheery wave, proving the old point that America is both really friendly and really dangerous.

The hostel was tired and empty, I was glad to be the only occupant of a six-bunk dorm. I should have stopped there, but as I was going off again soon, this was my only chance to see the famous Las Vegas Strip. I padlocked my locker and headed gamely towards the reception desk, manned by a kind and curvy Welsh girl who'd been in Vegas for six months.

May she be exalted forever, because when I asked her where to go to board the Deuces (double-decker tourist buses which cruise up and down the Strip 24 hours a day), I found myself quite unable to understand her answer.

Five times that blessed, patient girl explained to me where to pick up the bus, and five times I had to tell her I could hear what she was saying but could not take it in. I literally could not work out that, to get the bus, all I had to do was walk back up Fremont Street and turn right.

At heart, I would tend to say that most Autists are pretty blunt, straightforward people. The social graces can be mastered with effort but do not come automatically, and when the Autist gets tired, the façade of neuro-typical flexibility slips. In my case, any statement which is not blunt, clear, and black and white won't be understood; and any instruction to do anything more complicated than walk in a straight line will defeat me, or at the very least take me an inordinate time to process.

Slowly, slowly, like an amiable drunk trying to take directions, I worked out the route and headed off to the Strip.

Desert Mirage

Las Vegas is a Mirage. It's also a Bally's, a Bellagio, a Tropicana, a Flamingo and a palace of the Caesars, but mainly it's a mirage.

It would be too easy to call it cynical, corrupt, twisted, tawdry, neon-saturated, mob-influenced and lifestyle-wrecking, but it isn't that so much as a plain and simple illusion.

Paris, Venice and New York are not really here. The shopfronts barely conceal the casinos into which they open. I walked into a 24-hour Starbucks on Fremont Street, expecting to see a large coffee house. Instead I found a branch which would quite easily fit inside a medium-sized wardrobe, and behind it stretched aisle after aisle of glitzy one-armed bandits. The town is just a soulless machine clinically designed to hoover up money. Did vampires design it?

I really don't think I can recommend Vegas as a holiday destination for Autists. The neon light, garish shopfronts, constant muzak and noisy people ("we got so wasted last night and just sat around saying f*** a lot...") just aren't our thing, although the fictional Raymond Babbit somehow managed. On the double-decker bus, I sit behind a wrinkled Spanish crone with her young lover on the way there, and a desiccated David Bowie lookalike on the way back.

Walking towards Fremont Street, I am taking a picture of the Sahara when three black youths object to being accidentally included in it.

They think they're tough. I've lived in Glasgow and Lanarkshire for 13 years. The hardest eyes I ever saw were in Lanark, and I can smell the whiff of real violence in the air in an instant.

I stare at the ringleader, expressionless, and he backs off.

James Christie
March 13 2010

I'd taken the Deuce right down to the New York, New York Hotel and now I trudged back, looking at a fake Empire State Building, a fake Eiffel Tower and a fake Venetian campanile. At least Caesar's Palace and the Flamingo were real. Donny and Marie Osmond were appearing at the Flamingo, I photographed an easygoing pair of cage dancers at Harrah's, a group of seven not-so-magnificent latter-day hippies slouching in a corner of a small bridge and holding up a sign saying NEED WEED, WILL SMOKE, and a couple of girls out for fun gave me the glad-eye.

No, no time (and there were two of them, I wasn't Superman), it was pushing two in the morning and I had to be up by seven. I struggled on through the crowds of people, waves of sound and blaring golden, pink and purple neon signs, refreshed myself at a Walgreens store and evaded a drunken Oklahoman who reeled past me saying, "are you haviiing fuuun?"

Then I ran into the trio of black kids. Twelve years before, I'd been on a train in Glasgow late on a Saturday night, fit from many sessions at the Kelvin boxing club and feeling fed up to the back teeth with the West of Scotland's macho 'hard man' culture, when a red-faced kid who thought he was a tough guy tried it on with me. I stood up slowly and quietly proceeded to tell him what I thought of him, his lack of general knowledge, his prospects in life, his ancestry, his relations with his mother, and what I'd do to him if he laid a finger on me. I never even raised my voice, and then I called him out in front of his five friends, telling him that if he didn't put his money where his mouth was he'd lie a coward in his grave.

I always remember the way he just sat there with his mouth open. He'd tried to show off like a peacock in front of his friends, never thinking for a moment that the lanky blond in the seat in front of him wasn't an easy target, never thinking at all, and instead found himself being psychologically demolished and, worse, shown up as yellow in front of all his mates.

Red-faced, drink-fuelled yelling is not real aggression. A steady gaze and a white face is. The whitening of the skin means blood is being diverted to the vital organs in preparation for battle. If the aggressor sees his target showing these signs, he may hesitate.

Now, 12 years later, a black guy from Vegas was trying it on with me and I was just looking at him.

He hesitated.

"Aw, I was just ranking with you, man..."

"Go rank yourself," I muttered as he turned away.

The entire exchange had taken no more than 20 seconds. I got the Deuce back to Fremont Street and walked back to the hostel. I even talked to a nice lady from California on the way and found out she'd been in jail.

So what? At least she was pleasant company.

38

A date for breakfast

Friday March 12, 2010.

I always call it the last day. The day I made the crossing. I didn't lead a wagon train or drive an overloaded jalopy, but I went the same way. Crossing the Mojave to Los Angeles.

I woke up on time for the bus, broke my fast with free pancakes and coffee, and was quickly on my way. I remember the clear desert air, thin and cool, and breathing easy, as if it were yesterday, as I walked the 13 blocks back to the glitz and found my way to the Greyhound depot on South Main Street.

I'd long forgotten that I didn't need to go into Central LA. I could take the bus direct to Hollywood. It set out a little later than I'd expected, so I walked back across South Main and found a Starbucks. There was no free Wi-Fi there. Apart from my pancakes and coffee, nothing was free in Las Vegas. A hotel receptionist had explained that to me, too bored even to talk to me as soon as he realised I wasn't going to be spending any money.

So I was still blind. Juliet couldn't talk to Juliet. I wondered what was passing through her mind, turning on her computer and seeing nothing. I wondered what she would think of me if and when we met, and I had no answers.

Perhaps pilgrims on the mountain road to Calvary had felt the same way. I did not know, and the uncertainty, my inadequacy, twined deeper into my guts. What a fool I'd been to think I could do this. There was no future. I would be borne back into the past.

She had never let me down, though. That was the funny thing. Never a failure to respond. Sometimes no more than a happy face and a pair of initials. Other times bouncy and cheery, with exclamation marks galore. A kindness which had warmed me.

How very scared I was of everything, and in the end how very scared I was of her. This woman I knew, and did not know, and loved.

I got up. Time to take the bus to the place of broken dreams. I walked past the hungover revellers straggling up the street, past a bunch of kids playing basketball in the lot behind the Hotel Nevada, and found my bus. I sat down next to a girl named Precious and we headed out into the desert, climbing to 4,000 feet above sea level on California Highway 15 before beginning the long descent to the sea by way of Baker, Barstow and Dunn.

The plains were seared white, the rocks black as coal. I saw the cacti and the sagebrush, and faraway studs of fence poles deep in the golden pink desert. And I thought I glimpsed the faintest blue-white tinge on the horizon.

I didn't see the sign welcoming me to California, but the bus rolled into Barstow at lunchtime for a half-hour stop. I spotted a drive-thru Starbucks on the other side of the road and

To sleep, perchance to dream
To wake, and see the dream is truth

jog-trotted across, logging on to Juliet the Notebook's Wi-Fi and looking, once again, for the other Juliet.

There was a message in my inbox:

From: Juliet Landau
Sent: 12 March 2010 09:26
To: James Christie
Subject: Schrader Boulevard

Hi James.

I hope this reaches you! Do you want to meet up on Sunday for breakfast at 10.30? I got Drusilla's Redemption and look forward to reading it when I come up for air from all the TAKE FLIGHT stuff. My producing partner read it and loved it!!! He'd love to join us as well.

:)

Juliet

From: James Christie
Sent: 12 March 2010 12:42
To: Juliet Landau
Subject: Schrader Boulevard

Dear Miss Landau

In Barstow. See you for breakfast!

Best wishes

James

From: Juliet Landau
Sent: 12 March 2010 23:23
To: James Christie
Subject: Schrader Boulevard

See you then!
Juliet

See you then. The plain and simple words were like poetry. To meet a star on Sunset Boulevard one Sunday morning in March. Some moments come only once in a lifetime.

The bus went on its way to the coast, past the shining white planes at Edwards Air Force Base and the town of Mojave, baked quietly dry by the heat. We came over the San Gabriel mountains and there was Los Angeles, the hazy low-slung urban sprawl spreading down to the sea, topped with a high, close-clustered central set of skyscrapers.

The sunlit city with its sparkling spires.

Green and pleasant suburbs replaced dry desert and scrub as we dropped down into the San Fernando Valley. The real Candlewood Drive was close, and it was not far to go 'til Hollywood.

All the places I'd never seen, or thought I'd never see again. The violent, dreamlike city on the edge of forever to which I'd sent *Drusilla's Roses*, never expecting a reply.

A female passenger in her forties began to panic as we neared Hollywood Boulevard. She was intelligent, certainly. Neuro-typical, definitely, and had never travelled independently in her life. She'd always had a timetable and itinerary worked out for her in advance. She had never been out on her own until now, and all the atavistic fears I knew so well were crashing in on her for the first time.

The driver and I reassured her she would be able to pick up her connecting bus in Hollywood, and I was bemused to hear myself talking like the voice of experience, telling her it was quite natural to feel unnerved arriving in a strange city late'ish of an evening...

You don't know the half of it, lady, I thought. Hard for an NT. *Hell* for an Autist.

I left her by the correct bay to catch her connection and walked down to the hostel on Schrader, glancing at the palm trees on the sidewalk and the Hollywood Hills in the distance.

I was there, and the song was alive in my soul.

Two little guides I met on the way to Sunset

39

Smoke and mirrors

They say the past is another country, but I lived there and knew it well. The moments of which I was a part may one day be no more than fading images under dusty glass, but those old pictures captured the lives we truly lived. We were not a race of giants who walked in grace and did good deeds. We were not selfless or fearless. With all our flaws and foibles, we were only your fathers; and if we could say one thing to you, what would it be?

I was there. I lived and felt and loved. Read this and remember me.

Like the panicking lady on the bus, the tension was wrought like iron in my gut, but I guess my age gave me gravitas. I checked into the hostel on Schrader, scared a group of Yorkshire lads in the six-bed dorm with tales of the Los Angeles I'd known in 1989, and was pleased to learn that things were (apparently) safer in 2010.

I did not sit pompously in silent contemplation of my quest's conclusion, but went on a pub crawl organised by the hostel, hung around a couple of murky bars and ended the evening in a nightclub, hauling out some well-worn dance moves and gliding around as best I could in a pair of walking boots. A young Chinese-American girl took an interest and a couple of very well-built black ladies took me in hand.

Not bad for a 45-year old.

I had however assumed that, although I was a six foot four natural blond, I would simply be outclassed by hordes of tall, blond, unemployed 25-year old actors. All younger, better built and better looking than me.

Not so.

The clock ticked down to zero hour and I made my meticulous preparations for the rendezvous on Sunset Boulevard. On the Saturday morning, I got my hair trimmed at a barbershop on Hollywood and Vine. The young lady who cut my hair bounced brightly to her feet as I walked up to her. I almost expected her to say, "hi, I'm Debbie and I'll be your hairdresser!"

She looked at my hair, I asked her about blonds in Hollywood, and I'll never forget her answer:

"Hollywood's a strange place. It's all smoke and mirrors. There just aren't that many six foot four blonds around *anywhere.*"

"So," I said, shaping my words carefully, "in the land of smoke and mirrors, I am the real deal?"

"Yes."

I stood up. I'd always favoured shades of blue, and with autistic habit tended to wear one of several similar pairs of jeans and rugby shirts all the time. The shirt hung on a body much as lean and fit as it had been 21 years before, and if it's said that Los Angelenos were 'dark and golden-eyed,' then on that day I fitted the bill. The man who had not aged in the kingdom that worshipped youth.

I brushed my hand through the golden hair, paid my bill and went out to meet whatever destiny awaited me.

With the help of a free local map and the unstinting staff at the hostel's reception desk, I found out the route to the restaurant where we would meet, which Metro bus to take and what the fare was. I even did a dry run, familiarising myself with the rendezvous point.

Lastly, I found a rose. I'd like to say I climbed a mountain to find it, and plucked it from a far eyrie while fighting off a dragon, but it wasn't quite that difficult. There was a garden centre just south of the hostel on Sunset Boulevard. The centre shop had a fridge, and in the fridge were red roses.

Drusilla's roses.

I think my true motives only came clear to me then.

I begged the hostel staff for a bottle so I could keep the rose watered and alive for the night, then settled down to wait. The impossible was happening, the inconceivable at hand. Two weeks before I had been in a chilly Partick still becalmed in winter. Now I was amidst the palm trees of Hollywood, about to meet a star.

I definitely wouldn't need an alarm clock to wake up in the morning.

40

The best of days

The sun always shines in LA, and that day it shone for me. The lady driving the bus hoped the rose was for her.

"Not today," I smiled. "Not today."

I was on Sunset Boulevard by 9.30am. Best not be late on this of all days! I checked my bearings. A coffee house on my right, a black and silver edifice which looked like nothing so much as a flying saucer which had crashed to earth sideways lay ahead of me, and the rendezvous point was to my left.

Above and beyond, wreathed in green trees, were the Hollywood Hills.

I remember the cypress trees, tall as upright javelins, and the scent of fresh forest air.

A long way from Drumchapel.

People eddied past me. I kept the rose upright in its carrier bag, and watched, and waited.

My nerves were stretching me tauter than ever. I was opening myself up, letting my guard down and trusting another. That trust had been shattered in the past and although I knew there was no reason for it to happen again, my subconscious remembered and enjoyed reminding me what it felt like to have my faith crucified by someone I trusted.

Perhaps the Devil really would take his pound of flesh from me once again the way he – or rather *she* – had done 21 years before.

That was then. This is now.

She's never let you down.

Just wait.

And after a while, as well as waiting, I wrote:

Dear Miss Landau and the Sunlit City

They say all America looks for that sunlit city on the hill, where the sidewalk ends and the good life begins.

Perhaps there's a hint of Mom's apple pie in the air, malted milkshakes at the diner, the scent of coffee always on the brew; and that most delicate and fragile of things, the tinge of lost innocence in the air. Like seeing your first love as she was, before disappointment and disillusion changed her.

For some, Sunset Boulevard signals the end of dreams. It's the last stop of the trolley car, the red light at the intersection, the look on the doctor's face when he has to deliver terminal news.

And then again, sometimes not.

The message was thankfully clear. The hopeful trust I'd carried for a year, across an ocean and over 3,000 miles of hard road, was about to be fulfilled.

A small thing was going to happen. Of no interest to most, of curiosity to some, perhaps a subject of speculation to others.

From somewhere I smell the scent of roses, and I think I hear Drusilla singing softly in the distance.

The bus drops me off at the end of Sunset. I look up and see, not the house on Candlewood Drive, but the homes way up in the Hollywood Hills, well lit by the sun. I find myself smiling.

I wait for a while. I no longer feel tired or weary. Those aches and pains are the province of other, older men; and I am young again, as I was before.

I see a face in the crowd, coming closer. It is familiar.

Oh dear Miss Landau, it is so good to see you!

James Christie

March 17 2010

I remember she was dressed in blues and a scarf which shimmered like silk.

I remember her hair, raven black in the light.

I remember how I took her hand, and the way she smiled.

I remember it was the best of days, that Sunday morning in March on a boulevard west of Sunset.

The restaurant was full, so we breakfasted at another place. I don't know where it was. Perhaps on Melrose Avenue. Like Dru, Juliet was quiet, letting her 'producing partner' do the talking. He put a lot of store by fate and destiny. I demurred a little, reluctant to presume too much, but I agreed with him more than he knew.

The producer took the stage. A fellow Virgo, within a year of my age. Same British accent and shared cultural background.

"I'm sure you've got hundreds of questions," he concluded, "so I'll just pass you over now..."

I looked at her, and from behind her sunglasses she looked at me.

"How's your ankle?" I asked.

41

Victorian at heart

I think that broke the ice. I think, just for a second, Juliet Landau was completely flummoxed. I wasn't obeying the script and I wasn't asking the regular questions, but after six, maybe seven long years while fate, destiny or coincidence did its thing and slowly, slowly brought us together, I wasn't going to act like an ordinary fan at a convention.

It was not for me to boast of resurrecting Drusilla, or crossing America, or regale her with stories of sleeping in dorms or walking up to the Lincoln Memorial on a clear day. There were a thousand tales I could tell, but all I wanted to say, that day I sat with her, was:

I do not know who set the course, what latitude I did steer. I do not care how long it took, with how much pain and how much fear. I only know I needed come and stand before you, and say,

Remember me, for I am here.

She was so much shyer than I'd realised. Even I, the non-empathic Autist, would instinctively cut away from subjects which might upset her, and I lived in quiet fear, then and later, of hurting her without meaning to.

It was also unaccountably strange to sit with the living human counterpart of a presence I'd already known for months. To see a face for the first time with which I was already familiar. Drusilla Keeble and Juliet Landau. One and the same yet not the same, and time out of sync now realigning itself. I'd felt that on the way across, as the time zones separating us came down, seen the quiet presence of Drusilla out of the corner of my eye at odd moments when I was tired or distracted and now, sitting with Juliet, I began to notice how quiet she was too.

Even more strangely, the empathy I had for the fictional Drusilla had seemed to transfer itself to the real person when we began emailing each other, but what would happen now I'd met Juliet Landau in the flesh? Where exactly did the one leave off and the other begin?

I think the philosophical and psychological ramifications of an Autist dealing with a fictional character, her human alter ego and the Hollywood cult of celebrity all at the same time would need a book in itself. All I will say is they both seemed to share the sweet shyness I'd sensed in Drusilla and distilled into *Roses*, and Juliet and I seemed tentatively to make a connection.

There was the straight-backed carriage of the ex-professional ballerina, no doubt drilled into them unto death, and just like Drusilla as I had written her:

Drusilla still had the upright carriage of the rigidly-corseted Victorian lady and as she glided around the house, Giles was sometimes strongly reminded of his own grandmother, Edna, born in 1877.

(Drusilla 's Roses)

Drusilla had indeed been a Victorian, surviving into the present day courtesy of demonic immortality. Juliet Landau, although a woman of the modern age, had an almost Victorian quality of shyness and reserve, perhaps faintly echoing some of present-day America's Victorian character, '*Most Americans*,' as the former British ambassador to the US Christopher Meyer had said, '*believe that their country's actions in the world are intrinsically virtuous. The attitude of Britain's Victorians was very similar.*'

A superb actress, of that there was no doubt, but nor was there any doubt in my mind that Joss Whedon had seen the other qualities within her which made her perfect for the role of Drusilla; and somehow, 11 years later, a non-empathic Autist lacking social imagination had responded to those qualities, resurrected Drusilla and in the process restored himself.

It was certainly true that I had struggled to draw the other characters in *Roses* correctly, yet depicted Drusilla, the most difficult of them all, with staggering ease.

In a word, how?

Well, I was actually part-Victorian myself. My father was born into the British Empire in India, and briefly commanded a fort on the Khyber Pass in 1947. I had learnt the craft of cataloguing in my first post, where I restored a remote stately home's private library and in the process accidentally immersed myself in Victorian life and times. The house had been built between 1824 and 1828: unlike many buildings given over to the National Trust, it had remained in private hands until the 1980s. It was like a little bubble of the 19th century surviving into the 20th. I also got to know the laird's mother, born in the Edwardian era, still sharp as a tack in her eighties and regularly displaying Victorian/Edwardian manners in front of me.

So the library in which I had worked, once dusted off, re-shelved and re-catalogued, was much the way a girl born in 1840 would have seen it. The young, human Drusilla could have visited it and been shown round by the librarian, quite at ease with the manners of another time.

It had been a unique experience. For me the past was alive, immediate, vividly colourful and real. So when I came to write a character from that past, it was natural for me. Drusilla had been of the then-unpopular Catholic faith, and the landed gentry who had built the stately home had also been Catholic. Cardinal John Henry Newman had caused a monstrous ecclesiastical furore in 1845 by converting from the Church of England to the Church of Rome, and I remember cataloguing first editions of Newman's *Idea of a University* and *Apologia Pro Vita Sua*. I also have a strong, unfocused memory of seeing the illustrated plates in *The Dream of Gerontius*, and by no conscious means I could name, the beliefs, culture and debates of another age had seeped into my blood. I had been steeped in the knowledge of Drusilla's life and times, waiting until it was needed.

That was part of it, then. The Victorian author able to write the Victorian girl. The skill honed over 20 hard years of rejection and one failed Great Scottish Novel, all ready to peak with just the right stimulus, but that wasn't all of it. There was a missing factor.

Autists don't have much empathy. I should not have been able to feel for Drusilla, to care for her, sometimes to love her, but I had, and I'd done it easily.

Juliet Landau sat across from me, the person it seemed I'd been drawn to through time, over seas and across a continent to find, and she did not know how to ask the questions to which I could find no answers. Scotland and America. Partick and Hollywood. The celebrity and the man in the street. Only feet away from each other but gulfs apart. The isolation of the Asperger, not helped by the crash of my processor, which had been completely overwhelmed by it all.

But the trick to getting a character is finding the key which unlocks the puzzle, I've heard a certain actress say, and she went and did it in the end. By George, she went and did it.

Despite the meshing of cultures, it had been one fine surreal morning. I'd dropped off the edge of reality, come in on a wing and a prayer, reached the city on the edge of forever and she'd caught me before I fell; but it was only in the car on the way back to the hostel that she found the key.

Twice in ten years, I'd had women tell me (in some consternation) that they couldn't read me and couldn't work out what I would do next. I suppose that put them at quite a disadvantage. Some men may like to think they are strong, silent types, commanding and unreadable. As I understand it, many women let them salve their male egos by thinking this while using their womanly wiles to get their own way via subtle manipulation.

However, because I was on a radically different autistic wavelength, it looked like I really *was* unreadable. Some years earlier, I had just assumed that was the way things were, let my unreadability lapse into the file of personal fact and thought no more of it. I developed my social skills as best I could, dealt honestly and humorously with women, and occasionally got laid. Very occasionally.

In the car I conversationally mentioned that I was unreadable, and I'd swear I actually saw Juliet's ears prick up.

She turned round in her seat and looked at me, smiling. "I can get your emotions," she said.

The celebrity and the man in the street

42

The house on Candlewood Drive

How to follow that day of days? If I could have frozen a moment of time and remained within it forever, I would have chosen to stay that day on Sunset; but the world spun on (as it had to do) beneath the stars in their orbits.

Still high on a giddy mixture of fear, adrenalin and elation, I floated into the hostel's kitchen the morning after, found some coffee and eyed up my emails. There was one from my dear Miss Landau in my inbox (yay! as she would say) and I sent two to my workmates in Glasgow:

From: Juliet Landau
Sent: 14 March 2010 18:35
To: James Christie
Subject: Re: Redemption, roses, breakfast and posies…

Hi James.

It was a pleasure to meet you today!

Thank you for the wonderful books and the beautiful rose!

Best,

Juliet

From: James Christie
Sent: 15 March 2010 17:49
To: Ian MacRae
Cc: Marion Byrne
Subject: Redemption, Roses, breakfast and posies…

Hi Ian & Marion

Sometimes dreams can come true.

Best wishes

James

From: James Christie
Sent: 16 March 2010 19:14
To: Annette Monaghan
Subject: Juliet

Hi Annette

...Relieved I took the decision to answer Juliet's 'lost' email, otherwise all this would never have happened...

Bit emotional now. Crossed an ocean and three thousand miles of land to reach her, to reach this place, and now I am come down to the sea and it is done.

Best wishes

James

In some ways it surely was, but I still had the house on Candlewood Drive to see, so that Monday I struggled through the subway to Union Station. From there I took a slow train to a stop called Sylmar in the San Fernando Valley.

It was a long road up from Sylmar to Candlewood Drive and the buses were off that afternoon. However, I'd bought a straw hat at the Pueblo de Los Angeles opposite Union Station and carefully checked the local street signs in order to orientate myself so, twitchy with impatience, I decided to walk it.

I think it was about 90 degrees Fahrenheit, but I'd done heavy work in 100 and my body remembered. Like a worker ant, I crawled up the outlying northern edge of Los Angeles, the San Gabriel mountains looming on my left and the sidewalk dry and firm under my feet. After a couple of settling-in niggles the long muscles in my legs cleared out the kinks and I got into my stride.

Chaucer's pilgrims must have felt like this on the way to Canterbury. You could change the habits for jeans, the Kentish lanes for Stateside sidewalks, the cathedrals for suburban homes in secular days, and the date from the 12th century to the

21st, but the men you could not change. I walked in the steps of my fellow travellers, I knew how they felt and wondered what tales might be written of me.

It was about four miles, and I came over a rise mid-afternoon to see a young man standing on the grass by the verge. Quite tall and pretty lean, he was bewhiskered and casually dressed. His eyes were hidden by wraparound sunglasses and, judging by the way he leaned on his hoe, he was as laid-back as a classic California hippie.

A guide along the way.

"Do you know the way to Candlewood Drive?" I asked.

"Straight down there and first on the left."

I looked along the road, past the cypress trees and towards the line of hills.

"Sir," I said, "you will never know how grateful I am to hear that."

I saw the blue and white sign which said Candlewood Drive and let out a whoop. I walked up the slate grey road flanked by bungalows with great garages, a touch littered with black wheelie bins, shaded with short palms and long tall cypresses. Just another suburban street, not so far from Peyton Place or Pleasant Valley, picked off a Google map for its beautiful name.

I went on up to the end of the road, hung my sweaty shirt on the branch of a tree to dry, and took my time to savour the moment. Candlewood Drive. The street where Drusilla and the Scoobies had lived after the Fall of Sunnydale.

It was a hot afternoon, the Stars and Stripes hung straight and stiff from a nearby flagpole, and I had reached the road I thought I'd never see.

I stayed there quite some time. Then I walked back down to the stop at Sylmar like the hunter come home from the hill.

Candlewood Drive: the faraway street with the beautiful name

Sometimes you have to do the tourist thing ...

43

Right from the start

Ordinary life is untidy, and it truly seems that Allah does indeed weave the threads of men's destinies into many strange tapestries. If this were a tale of fiction, it would come neatly upon its end in one time, one place and one point; but as this tale is true, its tapestry has no one ending and many variations on its themes.

The Cyprus Film Festival had suddenly fallen apart and Juliet wasn't leaving the country, so I had not needed to run so fast for Los Angeles after all. I didn't give a damn. I'd reached her and that was all that mattered. Not only that, Juliet and her producing partner had invited me out to dinner so I extended my stay in LA. I'd burned out most of the adrenalin overload which had blighted our first meeting by walking up to Candlewood Drive, so we met again more successfully on the Wednesday evening. I broke out my better slacks and best blue shirt, ironed the ensemble to within an inch of its life and waited in the hostel's courtyard for my dear Miss Landau.

When her car arrived, her producer headed straight for reception and right past me. I adroitly slid to my feet, walked up to the car's window, and there she was again. I may have touched the window for a moment. There always seemed to be some barrier between us.

We ended up back at another restaurant, maybe once again on Melrose. Juliet was quiet so her producer and I made small talk. I was at ease with her reserve. The Drusilla with whom I'd lived had been very much the same. Quiet in repose of an evening, like jasmine flowering at night.

I'd planned to ask a more coherent set of questions, but she tired suddenly so I had to rush through them. First and foremost, though, I had to know, could this girl from the other side of the world really – somehow – read my emotions?

I tapped my chest, formulating the question logically.

"Can you really get in here?" I said, pointing at my heart. "I mean I'm very pleased about it, but you shouldn't be able to."

"Yes."

"How *long* have you been able to?"

I remember her eyes were a beautiful blue.

"Right from the start," she said.

Perhaps my eloquence had enabled her to do so, or perhaps I was reading too much into it. I'll never really know, but if I'd learned one thing over the long years it was that isolation was a mug's game, and Autists too often the mugs forced to play the game of isolation.

I've talked enough of the ineptitude, misunderstandings and loneliness that is too often the lot of Aspergers like myself. If I have made myself out to be a hero then have no doubt I am not, but the only way for us to change our fate is to step out on the road.

Like Drusilla, Juliet would sometimes converse with only a smile, a nod or a frown. On the way back to Schrader we had our last talk, agreeing to stay in touch, not knowing if there would be an end to it.

Perhaps it was part of the flipside of celebrity culture. The millions who think they know you. The few who actually do. The impossibility of trust and the souring of hope in Hollywood's goldfish bowl.

I do not know.

All I do know is that when we stopped and it was time for me to go, I held her hand for a moment. A strange look crossed her face. The knowledge of parting, I suppose, and the realisation that all too soon time and space would be bent out of sync again.

But to be young and know such moments. I would cross the world in a heartbeat to feel them once again.

44

Point Lobos

I took the early morning bus to Monterey on Monday March 22. Dawn was breaking over the Hollywood Hills when I left the hostel on Schrader. I looked along the boulevard as I crossed to the depot, searching out the cypress trees, knowing I had to walk away. I am very glad no-one could see the look upon my face.

Six men slept under the overhang by the entrance to the depot, and as the sun came up a big black man marshalled them to wakefulness.

"Alan! Anthony! Adam!"

He seemed disciplined, alert and intelligent. Snapping their names out quickly but not harshly, like an experienced drill sergeant rousing raw recruits at Pendleton. Yet he was hopeless and on the streets. I took his hand, wished him all the best, and he smiled. There's a bond on the road, where you might have to rely on a man as if he were your brother.

They melted away as the Puerto Rican clerk opened for business, and with the ruthlessness the traveller must also have, I turned my attention to the business of the day. Travelling to Monterey via Salinas and San Luis Obispo. A little town in California's Central Valley, home to America's first motel and the kind of place where everyone aspired to live behind a white picket fence.

In *Drusilla's Roses*, Xander had watched over an unconscious Drusilla as she slept in a bed with a brass bedstead. I'd had my doubts that such a traditional piece of furniture would often be found in modern, stylish California, but the hostel at San Luis Obispo had a single room going spare, complete with just such an item. A pleasant bolthole for the pilgrim on a night's retreat and a chance to catch up with myself.

I did so in a curious way, bumping into a girl from Hillhead in Glasgow and talking about the troublemakers I'd met at the organisation. They had left me with a deeply jaded view of some aspects of Scottish culture which had come over when I'd met Juliet, and I felt I might have been a bit unfair towards my own country.

"Don't be," she said. "I worked with one of *them*, too. Came in at nine, did one task, then got on the phone to moan to her mother for the next *hour*."

That seemed to sum it up. Deeply immature, small-minded, parochial and vicious people who seemed determined to bring everyone around them down to their level. A plague on any country and a plague on Scotland.

Cheered to find I was not alone in my views, I found my muse and assembled some words:

The Grapes of Wrath and the New Migrant Peoples

The timber-frame homes are neat and clean, the sidewalks quiet and leafy. There's a park in the centre of town and the buildings are the usual combination of red stucco tile and cream masonry paint.

There's a restored Amtrak station south of centre, with an interior of burnished mahogany. It hosts long silver trains running unhurriedly between Los Angeles and San Francisco. Couples hang out in parks, cars move quietly by. This town, and others like it, are planted amidst the Central Valley, one of the richest agricultural territories in the world. California itself is America's third most populous state. If it was an independent nation, it would be one of the world's top ten economies.

So in this and other small California towns, there seems to be good reason for the cars, the trains and the days to move unhurriedly by. No reason to query the sense of quiet, solid prosperity which hangs easy in the dry, calm air.

Yet, Dan Walters says in the Sacramento Bee *that,* "the *[California]* budget remains chronically unbalanced, state government is not noticeably smaller or more efficient ... California, with 12 percent of the nation's population, has nearly a third of the welfare cases" *and the California Taxpayers Association has just compiled a report contending that* "waste, fraud and mismanagement by state governors has cost taxpayers more than $18.9 billion since 2000."

Wikipedia (hopefully correctly) states that "California is facing a $26.3 billion budget deficit for the 2009-2010 budget year" *and makes the interesting point that a minority of prodigiously rich citizens are paying most of California's taxes. In 2004, according to Wikipedia,* "the richest 3 percent of state taxpayers paid approximately 60 percent of all taxes" *so while California remains rich in private, it's poor in public because the income of the super-rich is apparently highly dependent on capital gains via the stock market, and because of the credit crunch, these have been hit hard.*

Recession cannot truly hurt the very rich, but what about California's other 97 percent?

"What can I do to earn my pie?" *asked a lady standing at the kitchen island in a hostel just off a dusky sidewalk in one of those small, prosperous California towns. It brought to mind a scene from* The Grapes of Wrath, *where a man and his sons stop off at a roadside diner on Route 66, streaked with dust and smelling of sweat, not sure they'll make it across to the coast, trying to buy bread for ten cents, without a dime for a piece of penny candy. Banana cream, pineapple cream, chocolate cream and apple pie luxuries far beyond their reach.*

"What can I do to earn my pie?" *Perhaps that was the refrain of the migrant people heading west in the days of the Great Depression and Roosevelt's New Deal, making camp by the roadside at night. Tent cities created at dusk and torn down by morning, reverently leaving in shallow graves those who died, moving on towards the orchards and the production lines and the promise of work.*

Perhaps they ask the question again, now we are in the days of the New Depression and tent cities have appeared once more. Near Ontario east of LA, in Fresno and on the American River, just outside Sacramento. There may be new shallow graves.

California's unemployment rate reached 12.2 percent in late 2009, partly due to the foreclosure crisis and the slowdown in construction. A construction worker on holiday told me that the banks are hamstrung by foreclosed properties on their books and interest rates are too low, so there is too little lending, which leads to a stagnant economy.

Yet the tent cities have not burgeoned, that air of quiet prosperity has not departed, and although the health bill President Obama has just signed has not been nicknamed The New New Deal, perhaps it signifies for the average American that, even though his country may be bankrupt, his job prospects dire and his home under threat of foreclosure, he can have his piece of the pie in some security now.

James Christie
March 24 2010

A lot of self-appointed roadside sages talk a load of drivel about travelling in order to find themselves. I had known perfectly well before I set out that once the romance and adventure of the trip gripped me, and if I was able to get the hang of a foreign culture again the way I had before, I would indeed trawl some philosophical deeps; but I had not expected literally to find myself.

Nevertheless, there I was, that other me, sitting on the throw-covered sofa in San Luis Obispo's hostel that night, tapping away on a laptop somewhat larger than Juliet the Notebook.

He didn't look like me, of course. He was several inches shorter, dark-haired and half my age. Just through his first year of independent travel and trying to confirm his flight back to Heathrow. I'd been to Australia in 1989 while he'd been to

South America in 2010, but we were immediately on the same wavelength and simultaneously started picking each other's brains for fragments of intelligence about travel.

We bonded without fanfare and walked up to the Amtrak station the following day. He to take one of those sleek silver trains to San Francisco, I to hop a ride on a Greyhound to Salinas.

We stood by the portico of the station, midway between Greyhound stop and railroad track. The old man and the young, brought together for a brief moment.

"There were times," I said to him after a while, "that I wished I'd died out there. Gone out in my prime instead of coming back to all the slow humiliations life grinds you down with."

He nodded.

"I know what's coming for you," I said. "I don't want to tell you about it. They won't understand, those who never went out, and you won't be able to tell them. You'll never be able to tell them. Oh, you can talk and talk and talk, but you'd have more chance of describing the colours of the rainbow to a blind man."

I looked over at the town. I'd been in San Luis Obispo before. A ghost, sitting for two hours in the old Greyhound depot, now demolished, in the middle of the night, waiting for a connection between LA and San Francisco. Nobody had known I was ever there.

"The only thing I'll guarantee you," I went on, unburdening myself, "is that you'll never regret it. I've had regrets and plenty of them, but not for a day, not for an hour, not for a minute, did I ever regret going out. Regrets are for those who never go."

His train was coming in, so with a wink and a grin he went on his way. I was left waiting for the Greyhound, looking down towards Los Angeles, wondering why the fates had seen fit to send me out again yet leave me alive. I had not tired, I had not aged, I had not fallen, but nor, it seemed, had I loved. Now I was walking away, slowly and deliberately, from all I had found, and I did not know how long it would be until I saw her again.

The bus took me on up to Salinas and Steinbeck country, where I changed for the local MST service to Monterey and the hostel on Cannery Row, which didn't open until five. As it was four, I decided to indulge myself with a late lunch at the Bubba Shrimp Company on the Row. It seemed quite fitting. Forrest Gump dining at Bubba Gump's.

Most of California's oddballs seemed either to be working at or checking into the hostel. The man at the desk warned me about the danger of electricity pylons and of how non-organic food would shut down half my DNA, a guy called Rocky meditated in the dorm room for an hour at five o'clock the following morning, and when I wandered down to the Row (there were no canneries any more and the onetime factories had been given over to tourism) I ended up talking to a politely confused Chinese-American girl from the hostel who hadn't decided on her sexual orientation yet and didn't know who she was. By this point I wasn't too sure who I was either, so we were well suited to each other.

The Monterey Herald was delivered fresh to the beechwood table in the common room every day, and there I saw the historic headline:

OBAMA SIGNS HEALTH BILL

Fragments of a life: the day Obama signed the healthcare bill

It was March 24 2010 and, preoccupied with my own personal journey, I'd forgotten about the outside world's woes. We Autists can be a self-absorbed bunch, but at least I'd have more tales to tell. I'd seen Australia at the Bicentennial, San Francisco before the '89 quake and the Twin Towers pre 9/11. Now I was witness to the birth of America's public healthcare bill.

I couldn't find it in myself to feel elated, though. I'd helped an elderly lady with her bags on the bus to Monterey the day before. She turned out to be an actress who'd known Juliet when she was ten.

"She was intelligent and charming, and she loved to dance," she said.

She still is, I thought, *and she still does*.

Back to work. My heart might have been in Los Angeles rather than San Francisco, but I was hardly going to allow myself to descend into a sulk and miss Point Lobos, the last stop along the way and the original motivation for my Homeric odyssey. It was only four miles away, just south of Carmel:

Point Lobos

"Most men lead lives of quiet desperation and go to the grave with the song still in them."

(*Henry David Thoreau*)

'This man was evil through and through. Bald, heavyset and brutish, with the mottled cheeks of the heavy drinker, he was the product of old mining camps in the Sierra Nevada or rough bars on the San Francisco docks. He had been mean and vicious in life. In death, he was totally in thrall to his demon.

He smelled of week-old sweat and piss, and his fangs were very long. She couldn't stop looking at them.

Then she saw what he was going to do to her.

Even she shrank away in horror.

When it was over, he threw her out into the open. By pure

blind chance, it was still night. She lay by a forest path for a while, whimpering softly, terribly hurt.

After a while, she sensed dawn coming and blearily thought about just letting the sun claim her, but some flickering sense of self-preservation dragged her slowly to her feet.

She smelled sea air. The ocean was nearby. She had always liked sticks of rock at the seaside. There would be no sticks of rock for her today, not after what had happened to her, but she would go there anyway.

Bent over, lurching, gathering what rags of clothing and shreds of dignity she could, she made her way down to the beach.

Her body slashed with bite wounds, she had wandered along the coast near Monterey Bay at dawn, still wondering whether she should wait for sunrise and end it all.'

(Drusilla's Roses)

The MST bus dropped me off by the Chevron filling station just south of Carmel. Point Lobos State Reserve, the location for one of the most pivotal and upsetting chapters in Drusilla's Roses, *and the original inspiration for my journey across America, is less than two miles away along California Highway 1, and I'll have to walk the rest of the way there.*

A Mack truck whisks by me, a little too close for comfort. I remembered the joke I'd made several times before I'd left Scotland:

"I'll try not to get hit by a Mack truck..."

*Not long after I said that, in a coincidence too bizarre for fiction, I saw a Mack Truck (*sans *trailer) tooling down the long straight stretch of road which passes by Tinto Hill in the Upper Clyde Valley.*

Coincidence, omen, or sign of predestination? I do not know, but a picture of Point Lobos produced by Google during my search for a location had awakened Thoreau's song, left me with a feeling of quiet desperation that I would never see that place, and a sense of horror that all there was left for me to do was go to the grave with the song still in me.

But Drusilla's Roses *had been written, and like a sea captain who once again had a ship of his own I'd freed myself from my life of despair. The dream of reaching Point Lobos had become reality and the race was nearly run. Perhaps, though, the near-miss with the Mack truck had been a timely reminder of the danger of hubris, so I walked humbly down the last road to Point Lobos and Drusilla's beach. The place I thought I'd never see.*

The blue Pacific was to my right, blue as it had been in my dreams, blue as Juliet's eyes.

I came to the carved stone sign which told me I was there. I walked up to the entrance station.

"Have a good day," said the ranger after I bought a map from him.

"Good day to you, too" I said, and went on into Eden.

James Christie
March 27 2010

There is a place called Gibson beach at the south east corner of Point Lobos. It's not much. Just sea, rocks and sky. The Pacific as I remembered it with the sound of surf. Sparkling slabs of grey granite speckled with quartz forming headlands, reaching out to the sea. Monterey pines overhanging the shore. Wildflowers on the slopes. Seaweed and kelp littering the sand.

I renamed it Drusilla's beach, just for myself.

I took my time on the beach where Drusilla decided whether she would live or die, remembering the explosion of creativity that night in my flat which had brought me to this place, writing the chapter without plan or draft or thought. Raising up Joss Whedon's lost child and bringing her back. As she had wanted, and as it seemed I'd been selected – *chosen* – to do.

Drusilla's beach

It would be easy to write a Hollywood happy ending, where I became a beachcomber on Point Lobos and sat by the sea, happy in my soul, but it wasn't meant to work out quite like that.

Life can imitate art, and at much the same time as I'd been writing *Roses*, Juliet had also been writing a tale of Drusilla, set in Los Angeles after the Fall of Sunnydale and serialised in *Angel* #24-25. One of her themes had been the way people inadvertently re-enact the past, and that was what had happened to me.

I'd been across America on a Greyhound bus before, 21 years earlier on the way back from Australia. Admittedly, I had been going in the other direction, but I'd crossed the States by bus and met up with a girl in New York. I had written to her for a year from Down Under, from tents, in backpacker hostels and by the light of the Southern Cross.

When I got to New York, out on my feet and with scarcely a dime to spare, she turned on me, tearing me to pieces with words like "it's all just casual" and "it doesn't really mean anything."

I later found out that she was so mixed-up and confused about her identity that she ended up having a sex change. The last I heard, she had a small goatee beard.

You may wonder why I have little time for those who bail out of relationships, who seem unwilling to even try and reach some level of emotional maturity or consider the feelings of others, or who cite fear of commitment as an excuse to behave carelessly towards loved ones. If you wonder, imagine how it felt to keep the faith with someone for whom you cared, to whom you wrote every week for a year (no email then, every letter written by hand and sent by post), and whom you travelled overnight on buses to reach because you couldn't afford to sleep anywhere else. Imagine what it felt like to reach the original rendezvous point only to meet a selfish little monster who could not even be civil, and then tell me how I am supposed to feel.

It wasn't casual and, at the time, it did mean something.

The years went by. She had killed part of me, I just didn't die; but when fate, circumstance and my will sent me out on the road again, I was scared of what the next girl could do to me. More scared of her than anything else, because I knew I would have no defence if she turned on me.

Rationally, I knew this probably was not going to happen, but rationality is *not* the sole arbiter of our moods, even an Autist's.

That hour waiting on Sunset had been the longest of my life. Half crazy with anticipation. Half shaky with fear. But Juliet had changed the outcome and rewritten the past.

A happy ending?

Nope, still something missing.

45

Dog Easy Fox

Maybe those self-appointed roadside sages were not quite as full of it after all. I'd departed Drusilla's beach and walked up to the farthest pinnacle of Point Lobos, where it was just me, the Monterey pines and the sea.

The view seemed to beg the question of why I'd come, and demand an honest answer from me.

"All right," I said, either to myself or to God. "You've tasked me enough. You've put me on the road, punched me about and made me face myself.

"All right. I admit it. I don't like being alone, and I'm sick to death of being the good guy who does the right thing but then has to exit stage left while someone else gets the girl.

"I'm tired of being on the outside looking in, so go do something about it for a change.

"I've done enough."

It was a simple speech, perhaps trite and self-pitying, but that was how I felt. I'd had enough of people like Madame Scrooge and Nurse Ratched, of feeling like I wasn't good enough to reach the gates of the sunlit city, and I'd certainly had enough of being tortured by the organisation. Despite all that, I'd put myself on the line again and changed my future, but now that I'd *made* the change, I wasn't enjoying the thought of walking away and going back to my old life of desperation.

I knew that the only thing worse than all the heaven and hell I'd been through was the thought of isolation, and I wasn't the only one. Many adults with autism often end up stuck on the outside looking in. Others are overlooked or forgotten and develop mental problems.

In one terrible case, a young woman who had been living abroad with her parents moved back to Britain with them when she was 21 years old. She was adamant she wanted to cope with life on her own in Glasgow, so when her parents left the country she stayed on and tried to do so, but apart from some distant relatives she was alone in the UK.

She simply could not integrate herself into society and became more and more isolated, falling into clinical depression before finally being diagnosed with Asperger Syndrome.

Her fear of isolation led her to befriend unsuitable people and she nearly married a man 40 years older than herself. Although her relatives stopped her virtually on the way up the aisle she went on being socially gullible, befriending anyone who showed an interest in her and letting her flat (which was in a rough area) be used as a drink and drugs den by the local lowlifes.

They dragged her down to their level and she ended up in prison, where she continued to cling to anyone who seemed to like her.

After a series of mental breakdowns, she finally got proper support and moved to another part of the country. A relatively happy ending, but only after seven years of horror.

Although I hadn't befriended such patently unsuitable people, she and I shared the same fear of isolation and inability to avoid it. I'd certainly been willing to cross the world to make a connection because I knew that existing alone was still worse than the most vicious rejection any mixed-up girl could mete out.

I didn't enjoy the walk back to Carmel. It felt as if, despite my best efforts, I was being borne back by the tide.

He needed a drink, and by then so did I

From: James Doherty
Sent: 23 March 2010 12:03
To: Christie, James
Subject: RE: Sometimes dreams can come true…

Hi James

I'm looking forward to catching up with you when you get back. You've packed so much into a few weeks, can't wait to hear about it over a hot choc or two.

Speak with you soon Dog Easy Fox.

Jim

From: James Christie
Sent: 23 March 2010 16:39
To: James Doherty
Subject: RE: Sometimes dreams can come true…

Hi Jim

Look forward to it at that Starbucks in Renfield Street, perhaps, where *Drusilla's Roses* began. A lot to tell. Wonder what will be next?

Dog Easy Fox, inbound.

Best wishes

James

From: James Doherty
Sent: 24 March 2010 08:42
To: Christie, James
Subject: RE: Sometimes dreams can come true…

Safe journey home, my friend.

During my preparations for the trip, I'd resurrected a shortened version of my father's call-sign from the Second World War: Dog Easy Fox. It hadn't had much use, but I slipped it into an email I sent to Jim from Monterey and later found that it had become my nickname at the NAS while I was away.

As my date of departure from Newark was getting near, and as I did not much want to face another long and grinding bus trip back through the American West, I walked over to Pacific Grove (where the young Steinbeck had lived) and booked a night flight from San Francisco to Chicago on the Sunday. It was an old trick. Make progress and save the cost of a night's stay in a hotel or motel. I would take Saturday night off, stay at a Best Western and see Pier 39, which I'd missed the last time I was in town.

Anyone writing those words should not expect sympathy for feeling unenthusiastic about the prospect of such travels. Words like San Francisco and the Golden Gate have a much more romantic ring to them than Govan and the Clyde, but my focus and motivation were beginning to slip, now that I'd seen Point Lobos and Candlewood Drive.

And Juliet.

What was the watchword of bomber crews coming back from operations over Germany in World War Two, though?

Concentrate, concentrate. Junkers 88s often hung around British airfields, on the lookout for exhausted crews looking forward to landing and lowering their guard a bit too soon. I would feel pretty silly if I made some stupid mistake on the next to last day or so and managed to get myself sent home in a body bag after all.

So concentrate, and stop thinking about Los Angeles.

Concentrate and write:

They don't give a...

The Salinas Greyhound terminal was the usual drab mix of light green tile and faded brown counter. A couple of Mexican-

Americans with arched black eyebrows waited at the gate, the usual nutcase in a baseball cap and long pants wandered about repeatedly asking everyone if the San Francisco bus stopped at Oakland, and a sheriff's deputy waited patiently outside to put a couple of ex-convicts on board.

I'd heard ex-cons were sent on their way with a Greyhound ticket. Now I was seeing it for myself.

It was a long way from the days of chivalry described by Malory in Morte d'Arthur *(a favourite of the young John Steinbeck in Salinas) but a more truthful description of everyday life in small-town California than a modern-day Malory might have written.*

There's also the cream and red stucco style which is a hallmark of California, the bilingual signs in Spanish and English, the long rows of plants in the Salinas Valley's rich soil, and the hooded workers moving across the fields with slow and terrible concentration.

Big old telegraph poles support sagging electricity cables on the way out of Salinas, and I see an old blue Buick on a side road in sparkling condition, a piece of the past offered up for sale to a discerning buyer.

A pregnant girl from Santa Rosa with olive skin and chestnut hair stirs in her seat in the opposite aisle, lost in discomfort as the baby presses on her bladder. Nearby a rail-thin Rastafarian with razor-sharp cheekbones and a small beard talks in rhyme to nobody.

Everyday life? I guess this is it. But what do they think of the US national debt, the health bill, or the war in Iraq?

I'd tried to get the answer to some of these questions over the past month, but a chance conversation with a ginger-haired graduate from Ohio at the Monterey hostel finally, crudely, hit the nail on the head.

"They don't give a HOOT, man!" he said. "They don't know a thing about it!"

I was a bit staggered. He was mainly referring to his fellow students, but it was a straightforward reminder that, to put it mildly, not all Americans are reasonable, dispassionate observers and critics of their own society.

"They don't give a HOOT, man," the graduate said again. "I'm going out to get hammered!"

I felt like joining him, but I restrained myself. I had to be up early for the bus.

The last stop before San Francisco was Oakland. A buck-toothed kid sitting near me suddenly upped and said:

"I'm home, man. I'm so happy!"

He was one of the ex-cons. He'd been in prison for two years. I chivalrously wished him good luck as he got off the bus, but I doubt he gave a hoot about America's problems either. He was just glad to be home.

James Christie
March 28 2010

Missing her (not Drusilla)

I got into San Francisco at about 5pm, walked round a deserted Greyhound terminal on Folsom Street (it had all the charm and vitality of Folsom State Prison, Sacramento) and painstakingly orientated myself once again, finding my way through canyons of skyscrapers and jog-trotting up Columbus Avenue towards the waterfront.

Where autism handicapped me, it also supported me. Twenty-one years earlier, doling out my last cents, I had had to walk up to Nob Hill and Chinatown by the tracks of the trams. I had been easily able to do it then, and thanks to the Peter Pan gene nothing had changed.

I might have been 45 and fairly civilised, but when I walked into the Best Western on North Point Street, resplendent in rugby shirt with thistle motif, muscles slightly pumped up from the pleasant exertion and with the typically autistic masked, no-nonsense look on my face, I'd swear a little ripple of unease went through the Americans in the lobby.

Although we were all middle-aged tourists together, *they* were buffed, polished, slightly paunchy, comfortably-off and middle-class. They all carried suitcases. *I*, on the other hand, looked like a backpacker in a bad mood who'd just got off the bus and walked through the wrong door.

I went over to the clerk at the reception desk, looked down at him and explained I'd made a reservation. He started talking about credit cards and down payments and other overcomplicated twaddle. I let him ramble on for a while, then I raised an eyebrow and brought him to a halt.

"Okay, pilgrim," I said. "Let's go back to basics. You give me room, I pay you money. *Capisce?*"

Relieved he wasn't going to be mugged, he handed over the passkey smartcard thingummy, I dropped my pack in my room and went off to explore. I did so for a while, walking along the waterfront amid the tourists and the entertainers. A guy hiding in a trash bin who jumped out like a jack-in-the-box. Another holding a sign saying he need cash for alcohol research. My heart didn't really seem to be in it, though, which was ironic as San Francisco should have been the one place in which I'd left it.

I ended up at a rather-too-expensive restaurant at the end of Pier 39, looking out at the twilight vista of Golden Gate and Sausalito, feeling like I'd lost my best friend. A mood I couldn't shake, even though I had no right to feel it.

I'd worked out that the best way to reach the airport for my Chicago flight on the Sunday afternoon was via the Bay Area Rapid Transit system, so I slept dreamlessly at the Best Western that night and went to see the Golden Gate Bridge the next day.

If Drusilla slept beside me that night, I did not know it. She had come a long way with me and been a better friend than most. Juliet's producing partner had even said Drusilla was my character now. I couldn't presume upon that, but during our first meeting, he'd also asked me one question about Drusilla which, amid the tumult of the day, had virtually gone astray. Now that I had a bit of time to think, it was coming back to me.

What called to you?

I'd already speculated that my quasi-Victorian experience had helped qualify me to write about someone born in 1840. I'd wondered how I'd managed to feel so much empathy for her when by rights I shouldn't have been able to; and I'd been very pleasantly surprised to find that Juliet seemed to be able to read my emotions.

Those queries and fragments of insight were only parts of the puzzle, though. I had not delved right down to the depths of my id and found the answer. I hadn't really had the time. I'd been too busy flying the B-17 or stealing the *Enterprise*, you might say, to allow myself the luxury of introspection.

But now I had a moment.

Why had I loved her so much?

And what of her human alter ego?

There weren't even that many male writers who could write women well, and there was no question that it was particularly hard to get Drusilla right. Yet I had done so, and made it look as easy as falling off a log.

Sure, Dru had *called* to me. That was undeniable. But what had made me *reply* so strongly, even passionately?

What had struck such a chord?

Not once in the last year had I considered that question. I'd had a vampire flatmate for six months, corresponded with a Hollywood film star, gone on a quest across America and found the Holy Grail thrice over, but I'd always tried to keep my feet on the ground and not wander up my own arse into a warm, wet world of literary pretentiousness. Instead of waiting for my muse, I'd been more likely to go sit in Starbucks with my Pukka Pad.

My Vulcan/autistic mind was quite a computer, though. Ask it a question and, sooner or later, it would chunter out the answer. All that week, while I had been making a mythic rendezvous on Sunset, following my guide along the way to Candlewood Drive and finding myself at Point Lobos, my subconscious had been trying to ascertain the answer to that question. Slowed down by my underpar processor, it had nevertheless gamely worked out what had been going on all the time; and as I stood at a bus stop on the way to the Golden Gate, it finished its calculations and presented me with the answer.

We were the same, Dru and I. Underneath the façade which for all I knew had struck fear into the hearts of the tourists in the lobby of the Best Western, I was just like the human behind the demon's face. Just as shy, just as lost and just as alone. She had not found me. We had found each other.

No wonder I could feel Drusilla's emotions, and no wonder Juliet could get mine.

I wandered round the Golden Gate tourist facilities, not paying much attention to the most beautiful bridge in the world, away in a world of my own.

Around and about the Golden Gate, away in a world of my own

Mirror image

46

Eighty-sixed

Jack Kerouac might have come to his end on Adler, or so a strange street sign said to me outside the City Lights bookstore but the store itself, founded in 1953 by the poet Lawrence Ferlinghetti and Peter D Martin, seemed happy and wealthy, which considering the bleak fate of many independent bookshops the world over, was really saying something.

I was able to drop briefly by on the way to the airport, belatedly reflecting that Drusilla would probably enjoy having Beat poetry read to her, before taking the Powell-Mason cable car down to the BART station on Market Street.

As the car rattled down the hill, I managed to get to the tiny observation platform at the rear and enjoy my one chance to feel the juddering flight of the San Francisco cable car for real. The brakeman, like me, seemed not to be in too good a mood, but when we ground to a stop on Powell and Market, I found a quip in my repertoire.

"Good trip," I said. "Missed it first time, 21 years ago."

He loosened up a bit.

"Come back sooner next time!"

I hope to.

BART shot me out to the airport with nary a rattle, I orientated myself without too many wrong turns and found my gate, the number of which felt like a fitting comment on my mental state.

Eighty-six.

I was eighty-sixed all right. Tired and glum and gloomy, on the road back from the greatest journey of my life and in no mood to do more than mope around at the nearby coffee shop.

I missed her.

Not Drusilla.

Only solution, write something:

The Thousandth Man and his Limitations

"Nine hundred and ninety-nine can't bide
The shame or mocking or laughter
But the Thousandth Man will stand by your side
To the gallows-foot – and after!"

(Rudyard Kipling)

Jack Kerouac was at his end on Adler, the late cable car was playing its night song on the way downtown from Nob Hill, and Ginsberg may have been gone but, in San Francisco, the Beat still went on.

But not for me.

I would be hopping a night flight to Chicago, there to stay with my long-suffering cousin, before taking a familiar and gruelling Greyhound bus trip to Newark airport and then home.

I sat waiting for my flight and wondering just what it had all been for. What, indeed, had made me walk 5,000 miles and more...

I stopped. I couldn't get the words out properly. I felt like a Beat poet stoned on marihuana and just *not getting it together, man*. Juliet's image stared at me from the desktop, so I shut it down.

I drank too much coffee and stood next to an off-duty cop when the call came to get in line for the plane. When I mentioned I'd come over from the East Coast on a bus, he just said:

"Sheesh!"

Jack Kerouac at his end on Adler,
with James Christie not far behind

Not the most eloquent of comments, but it just about summed up my achievement.

My cousin Keith was once again a lifesaver, with a welcome, a laundry, free Wi-Fi and a bed. I tidied up the order in which my articles had been submitted to the NAS Facebook page with the help of a nice young lady from the NAS London office, and prepared for a 17-hour Greyhound bus trip back from Chicago direct to Newark International Airport, driving through the night to arrive there at 11.30am for my 7.35pm. return flight.

Once all the details had been dealt with there was nothing else to do except take another look around Chicago. In one sense, I was going home. In another sense, I was distancing myself, time zone by time zone, from the place I would rather have been.

I walked across the main concourse of Union Station on the morning of March 30. It was Juliet's birthday, and I looked at the screens showing departure times of the great Amtrak trains, heading out across America to all points east and west. There was the *Southwest Chief*, leaving for Los Angeles, and there was I, going in the other direction.

From: James Christie
Sent: 29 March 2010 22:18
To: Juliet Landau
Subject: Happy birthday!

Dear Juliet

Three time zones distant and getting further away all the time, but glad I'm able to wish you a happy birthday.

Have a good day tomorrow and take care. I hope you'll like your present.

Best wishes

James

From: Juliet Landau
Sent: 30 March 2010 09:38
To: James Christie
Subject: Re: Happy birthday!

Thank you James for the birthday wishes and the beautiful present!
I love it!

Best,

Juliet

From: James Christie
Sent: 30 March 2010 11:16
To: Juliet Landau
Subject: Re: Happy birthday!

Dear Juliet

I'm very glad you liked the present.

Just like to say, it's been the best month of my life, and you're the
best gal in all the world.

Best wishes

James

From: Juliet Landau
Sent: 31 March 2010 21:04
To: James Christie
Subject: Re: Happy birthday!

:)

Juliet

Travellers live in a state of accelerated change, frequent uncertainty and constant adjustment to new places and people. As a result, we experience time differently. A week can feel like a month and a year a decade. Then there is the crashing return to normality and the re-establishment of regular routines. It isn't necessarily an ordeal, but the traveller returns aged and altered by the experience to friends who have scarcely noticed he's been away.

I'd had a life-changing month and now it was time to sum it up, but I couldn't find the words.

Well, sitting for 17 hours on a Greyhound bus, half asleep and half awake, listening to the green disinfectant slosh around in the loo at the back, would certainly give me a long, long stretch of uninterrupted time in which to work out what to say.

I hunkered down on the floor of the Greyhound terminal with a scared Mexican girl and a couple of amiable Honduran labourers who didn't know where Scotland was. I wasn't expecting any particular problems but I wanted to make sure I was in a good position to board. Technically, Greyhound was supposed to provide another bus if too many passengers turned up for a scheduled service, but this might be the one day when no spares were available. When I was filling out my ESTA questionnaire a month – or was it a year? – earlier, I'd also noticed one of the questions had asked whether I had ever departed the US even *one day* later than I should have. I got the impression that if I didn't obey America's laws absolutely scrupulously, they might not let me back in again.

Paranoid?

Perhaps, but this was the post 9/11 era. O brave new world, tied up with the war on terror and legislating itself to death like a snake swallowing its own tail.

I found my seat, prayed they wouldn't lose my rucksack, and did indeed spend the next 17 hours thinking and trying to find the words.

I remember something about changing at Cleveland and briefly breakfasting in Pennsylvania before blearily leaving the bus at Newark and groping my way to the train for the airport. As I waited on the platform a great double-decker train bound for Florida came in and I found myself staring at a little old lady in a window seat. She nodded to me gravely as the train pulled out and I raised my hand to her as she went. The last guide along the way and the most dignified of partings.

After that, there was nothing else to do except go to my gate and wait for departure, and as I waited, I came to my conclusions.

Drusilla had been my most constant guide along the way, giving me the empathy I needed to write *Roses* and restoring my faith in human nature. She'd been a wonderful flatmate, too, and I didn't know what I'd do without her around.

Then there'd been her human alter ego, Juliet.

There are sirens who lure ships onto the rocks, but then there was the song of the muse, which could make a man walk 5,000 miles and more. And not just every man, but Kipling's Thousandth Man, who would stand by her side to the gallows-foot and after.

Years before I'd been diagnosed autistic, a friend of my father with a personality-profiling business had analysed me. I'd forgotten what he'd found, but now it came back to me.

"At heart, James is like Malory's parfit gentil knight," the profiler had said to my father. "Quite out of place in this world."

A gentil knight. Still able to go on a quest, even in this day and age.

It looked like those blasted roadside sages were right after all. I had forgotten who I really was, and now I knew.

No wonder I had liked *Buffy*, with its tales of Arthurian chivalry and valour, so much. I was a bit of a Scooby myself.

I suppose Drusilla had known too, and sought out the one man in the world willing to redeem her.

Like me, though, Dru had her limitations. And once the tales had been told, it was not she who called the man across the sea to return the words to their keeper.

But she was my guide, as I went in search of my muse and of myself.

Drusilla's Roses had led me to the Rose. To the one girl in all the world who could get my emotions and bring out the best in me. Who'd been worth every moment of the time I'd put into planning and making the trip.

And I'd do it again in a heartbeat, even if I had to walk.

Now I'd be able to finish my article:

The Thousandth Man and his Limitations

"Nine hundred and ninety-nine can't bide
The shame or mocking or laughter
But the Thousandth Man will stand by your side
To the gallows-foot – and after!"

(Rudyard Kipling)

Jack Kerouac was at his end on Adler, the late cable car was playing its night song on the way downtown from Nob Hill, and Ginsberg may have been gone but, in San Francisco, the Beat still went on.

But not for me.

I would be hopping a night flight to Chicago, there to stay with my long-suffering cousin, before taking a familiar and gruelling Greyhound bus trip to Newark airport and then home.

I sat waiting for my flight and wondering just what it had all been for. What, indeed, had made me walk 5,000 miles and more?

To unshackle myself from Thoreau's life of quiet desperation?

Partly, yes. I had seen the pictures of Point Lobos last year which had certainly unleashed within me a desperation to escape from that quiet life of office routine before it was too late.

To show what (with the proper help and support) autism sufferers were capable of?

Yes, and I hope I have done so.

To publicise the Autism Bill?

Again, partly yes, and I hope I have influenced some.

But that wasn't really the heart and soul of it all, was it?

What really did make me get up and go on when I wanted to stop? What made me break myself to sleeping in dorms and travelling through the night on Greyhound buses, standing up to all the uncertainty and the fear and the change?

Perhaps it was that vital spark, that spirit which makes us all, aspie and typical alike, push the envelope of our limitations.

Or maybe it was simpler than that. The need to go into battle once more before it was too late. The need of the knight to stand before his lady one last time, before accepting the fading of the light.

All for you, Miss Landau!

Best gal in all the world.

James Christie
April 1 2010

47

I see something!

From: James Christie
Sent: 01 April 2010 12:43
To: James Doherty
Cc: Carol Evans
Subject: RE: The Thousandth Man

Hi Jim and Carol

This should be the last one – another deeply emotional piece and possibly a bit overdone, but, well, that's how it felt.

Waiting in the terminal at Newark now, at the end of a dream.

Best wishes

James

From: James Christie
Sent: 08 April 2010 21:11
To: Juliet Landau
Subject: RE: Time, sunrises and sunsets…

Dear Juliet

The bus had a near miss with a Mack truck near Cleveland, I filed the last blog from the airport, watched *Forrest Gump* on the plane and felt a bit like him when I arrived back.

Everything is the same, yet everything is different…

With my best wishes

James

I could talk forever of synchronicity, destiny and fate, but perhaps it's best to leave the last word to someone else.

I came back to empty customs halls and the 'old toun' on the Clyde, with tales of westering I could not tell and memories of sunlit days I could not share. All too soon I found myself back before my office door. On its other side my desperate life awaited me, but also my own Scoobies. The best of friends who, together with Jim, had supported me so well.

I took a breath and walked through the door. There was silence for a moment, then some clapping and quiet words of congratulation.

Perhaps my tale should have ended there, but a certain raven-haired vampire had other ideas.

Many threads may weave tapestries most strange: the seasons, the signature and the lady's colours, carried all the way to LA

Drusilla's Roses had not been the end of the story. No sooner had I despatched *Roses* to Hollywood and tried to put Drusilla out of my mind than my subconscious had coughed up a continuation. Dru had refused to be silenced, virtually dragged me back to the PC for the sequel and made me write *Drusilla's Redemption*, in which Dru and Xander went to London to work for the Council and ended up in the Congo, Africa's heart of darkness, fighting a primal superslayer, unearthing the origins of the slayer line and enabling Drusilla (like Spike and Darla) to redeem herself.

I hadn't known whether I could pull off the miracle twice. The wells of emotional intelligence had already been ebbing, but I'd done it. *Drusilla's Redemption* had been edited by Meltha and sent to Juliet Landau just weeks before I took flight, and the last part of the trilogy, *Drusilla Revenant*, had been assembling itself in my mind all the way across the continental United States.

Must a fool always rush in where a wise man fears to tread?

Probably.

Just after I finished *Redemption*, I'd watched an episode of *Buffy* which I'd seen many times before, but this time it was as if, now that the ferocious concentration of Asperger focus had been calmed and the second story completed, the magic box in the back of my head had declared itself ready to embark upon a third instalment.

Back in 1936, a former heavyweight champion called Max Schmeling had been lined up as cannon fodder for the up-and-coming contender, Joe Louis. Schmeling, however, had not been willing to end up as a KO victim on the new-kid-on-the-block's record. He watched every piece of film of Louis fighting he could find and analysed it, looking for flaws in Louis' style. Little imperfections no one would see at a casual glance.

"Stop the film," he would say over and over again. "I see something."

With the benefit of Asperger focus, I didn't even have to work that hard. Three days after finishing *Redemption*, watching a certain *Buffy* episode with a dispassionate eye, I saw something.

Joss Whedon's unfinished story arc. The key with which I could turn the Buffyverse inside out.

Against all the odds, Schmeling had pulled off an upset and KO'd Louis. Could *Drusilla Revenant* complete Whedon's arc and do much the same? In *Roses*, Drusilla had taken a swim off Gibson beach to let the salt water help heal her wounds. Then, sleek and shockingly beautiful, she had risen from the waters like a dark Aphrodite and gone in search of her white knight. Taking a Joss Whedon story arc forward might have seemed like David taking on Goliath, but I didn't think Whedon would actually kill me for such blasphemy, so why not guide my lost lady a little further along the way to Avalon? Once *Revenant* was ready, there was a chance the Drusilla trilogy could be published. Jim had also suggested I write a book about my real-life trip to inspire other Autists. I liked the idea. I'd walked round the National Steinbeck Center in Salinas, seen *Rocinante* (the old van in which Steinbeck crossed America), and the same thought had occurred to me.

A couple of months later, I had a submission ready for a publisher, provisionally entitled *Dear Miss Landau*. I sent it to the NAS for editing and when it came back, I was surprised to see they wanted to add the words 'it's a love story' to the text.

"I can't do that," I griped to Marion, one of my colleagues, who was both wise and beautiful. "I'm still in touch with Juliet. What the hell's she going to think if I send her a copy of the submission and she sees *that*?"

Marion looked at me, slightly surprised.

"We all thought it was a love story," she said.

ACKNOWLEDGEMENTS

With acknowledgement to the works of *Angel*, the BBC, *Buffy the Vampire Slayer*, Alistair Cooke and Harold Evans, Lee Cronin, Helen Fielding, F Scott Fitzgerald, Ian Fleming, DC Fontana and Laurence N Wolfe, Temple Grandin, Lynsey Hanley, Kate Hodal, Barbara Jacobs, John Keats, Ken Kesey, Stephen King, Rudyard Kipling, Juliet Landau, Christopher Meyer, Nicholas Meyer, Monty Python, the National Autistic Society, *Never Say Never Again*, *New Scientist*, Leonard Nimoy, *Rain Man*, *Scotland on Sunday*, *Star Trek*, John Steinbeck, Sylvester Stallone, *The Daily Record*, *The Mail on Sunday*, The *Sunday Herald*, The *Sunday Mail*, James Thurber, Henry David Thoreau, *Top Gun*, Joss Whedon and Zillagirl.

PHOTOGRAPHIC ACKNOWLEDGEMENTS

Author portrait (front cover and frontispiece) by Richard Campbell.

Mr Spock montage (page 3) by William Kay.

Juliet Landau photographs (cover, frontispiece, pp.63, 97, 121, 181 and 210) by Deverill Weekes. All photographs of Juliet Landau used with her kind permission.

All road-trip photographs by James Christie.